# California Standards
# Enrichment Workbook

**McDougal Littell**

# *World History*

## Ancient Civilizations

### California Consultant

Neal Cates
*Long Beach Unified School District*
*Lakewood, California*

**McDougal Littell**
A DIVISION OF HOUGHTON MIFFLIN COMPANY

**ART CREDITS**
**24** Ancient irrigation systems. Illustration by Peter Bull; **114** Mayan hieroglyphs. Museo
Nacional de Antropologia, Mexico City. © Giraudon/Bridgeman Art Library.

**ACKNOWLEDGMENTS**
Excerpt from *The Analects of Confucius,* translated by Simon Leys. Copyright © 1997 by
Pierre Rychmans. Reprinted by permission of W. W. Norton & Company.

History-Social Science Content Standards for California Public Schools reproduced by
permission, California Department of Education, CDE Press, 1430 N Street, Suite 3207,
Sacramento, CA 95814.

ISBN 13: 978-0-618-53140-0    ISBN 10: 0-618-53140-8

Printed in the United States of America.

23 24 25  2266  20 19 18
4500747693

# Contents

How to Use This Book . . . . . . . . . . . . . . . . . . . . . . . . . . . . . . . . . . . . . . . . . . . . . vi
Grade 6 California History-Social Science Content Standards . . . . . . . . . . . . . . . . . . . . . . . . . . . vii
California History-Social Science Analysis Skills Standards, Grades 6–8 . . . . . . . . . . . . . . . . . . . . . x

## QUICK PREP

Major Eras in World History . . . . . . . . . . . . . . . . . . . . . . . . . . . . . . . . . . . . . . . . . . .1
Major Empires . . . . . . . . . . . . . . . . . . . . . . . . . . . . . . . . . . . . . . . . . . . . . . . . . . .2
Major Geographic Features . . . . . . . . . . . . . . . . . . . . . . . . . . . . . . . . . . . . . . . . . . . .3
Major Figures in Ancient History . . . . . . . . . . . . . . . . . . . . . . . . . . . . . . . . . . . . . . . .4
Major Events in Ancient History . . . . . . . . . . . . . . . . . . . . . . . . . . . . . . . . . . . . . . . .6
Major Religions . . . . . . . . . . . . . . . . . . . . . . . . . . . . . . . . . . . . . . . . . . . . . . . . .8
Major Inventions in Ancient Times . . . . . . . . . . . . . . . . . . . . . . . . . . . . . . . . . . . . . . .9
Government and Economic Systems . . . . . . . . . . . . . . . . . . . . . . . . . . . . . . . . . . . . . .10
Key Terms and Names . . . . . . . . . . . . . . . . . . . . . . . . . . . . . . . . . . . . . . . . . . . . .12

## CA STANDARDS: REPORTING CLUSTER 1: WORLD HISTORY AND GEOGRAPHY: ANCIENT CIVILIZATIONS

6.1.1    **The First People**
         Review . . . . . . . . . . . . . . . . . . . . . . . . . . . . . . . . . . . . . . . . . . . .15
         Practice . . . . . . . . . . . . . . . . . . . . . . . . . . . . . . . . . . . . . . . . . . . .16
6.1.2    **The First Communities**
         Review . . . . . . . . . . . . . . . . . . . . . . . . . . . . . . . . . . . . . . . . . . . .17
         Practice . . . . . . . . . . . . . . . . . . . . . . . . . . . . . . . . . . . . . . . . . . . .18
6.1.3    **Learning to Use the Environment**
         Review . . . . . . . . . . . . . . . . . . . . . . . . . . . . . . . . . . . . . . . . . . . .19
         Practice . . . . . . . . . . . . . . . . . . . . . . . . . . . . . . . . . . . . . . . . . . . .20
6.2.1    **Early River Civilizations**
         Review . . . . . . . . . . . . . . . . . . . . . . . . . . . . . . . . . . . . . . . . . . . .21
         Practice . . . . . . . . . . . . . . . . . . . . . . . . . . . . . . . . . . . . . . . . . . . .22
6.2.2    **Early Centers of Culture**
         Review . . . . . . . . . . . . . . . . . . . . . . . . . . . . . . . . . . . . . . . . . . . .23
         Practice . . . . . . . . . . . . . . . . . . . . . . . . . . . . . . . . . . . . . . . . . . . .24
6.2.3    **The Role of Religion in Ancient Culture**
         Review . . . . . . . . . . . . . . . . . . . . . . . . . . . . . . . . . . . . . . . . . . . .25
         Practice . . . . . . . . . . . . . . . . . . . . . . . . . . . . . . . . . . . . . . . . . . . .26
6.2.4    **Hammurabi's Code**
         Review . . . . . . . . . . . . . . . . . . . . . . . . . . . . . . . . . . . . . . . . . . . .27
         Practice . . . . . . . . . . . . . . . . . . . . . . . . . . . . . . . . . . . . . . . . . . . .28
6.2.5    **Egyptian Art and Architecture**
         Review . . . . . . . . . . . . . . . . . . . . . . . . . . . . . . . . . . . . . . . . . . . .29
         Practice . . . . . . . . . . . . . . . . . . . . . . . . . . . . . . . . . . . . . . . . . . . .30
6.2.6    **Egyptian Trade in the Ancient World**
         Review . . . . . . . . . . . . . . . . . . . . . . . . . . . . . . . . . . . . . . . . . . . .31
         Practice . . . . . . . . . . . . . . . . . . . . . . . . . . . . . . . . . . . . . . . . . . . .32
6.2.7    **Hatshepsut and Ramses**
         Review . . . . . . . . . . . . . . . . . . . . . . . . . . . . . . . . . . . . . . . . . . . .33
         Practice . . . . . . . . . . . . . . . . . . . . . . . . . . . . . . . . . . . . . . . . . . . .34
6.2.8    **Ancient Kush**
         Review . . . . . . . . . . . . . . . . . . . . . . . . . . . . . . . . . . . . . . . . . . . .35
         Practice . . . . . . . . . . . . . . . . . . . . . . . . . . . . . . . . . . . . . . . . . . . .36
6.2.9    **The Beginning of Written Language**
         Review . . . . . . . . . . . . . . . . . . . . . . . . . . . . . . . . . . . . . . . . . . . .37
         Practice . . . . . . . . . . . . . . . . . . . . . . . . . . . . . . . . . . . . . . . . . . . .38

| | | |
|---|---|---|
| 6.3.1 | **Origins and Impacts of Judaism** | |
| | Review | 39 |
| | Practice | 40 |
| 6.3.2 | **Teachings and Central Beliefs of Judaism** | |
| | Review | 41 |
| | Practice | 42 |
| 6.3.3 | **Characters from the Torah and Jewish History** | |
| | Review | 43 |
| | Practice | 44 |
| 6.3.4 | **Migrations of the Jewish People** | |
| | Review | 45 |
| | Practice | 46 |
| 6.3.5 | **The Jewish Diaspora** | |
| | Review | 47 |
| | Practice | 48 |
| 6.4.1 | **The Greek City-States** | |
| | Review | 49 |
| | Practice | 50 |
| 6.4.2 | **Government in Ancient Greece** | |
| | Review | 51 |
| | Practice | 52 |
| 6.4.3 | **Direct and Representative Democracy** | |
| | Review | 53 |
| | Practice | 54 |
| 6.4.4 | **Greek Literature** | |
| | Review | 55 |
| | Practice | 56 |
| 6.4.5 | **The Persian Empire** | |
| | Review | 57 |
| | Practice | 58 |
| 6.4.6 | **Athens and Sparta** | |
| | Review | 59 |
| | Practice | 60 |
| 6.4.7 | **Alexander the Great** | |
| | Review | 61 |
| | Practice | 62 |
| 6.4.8 | **The Greek Legacy** | |
| | Review | 63 |
| | Practice | 64 |
| 6.5.1 | **Early Indian River Cultures** | |
| | Review | 65 |
| | Practice | 66 |
| 6.5.2 | **The Aryan Invasions** | |
| | Review | 67 |
| | Practice | 68 |
| 6.5.3 | **The Roots of Hinduism** | |
| | Review | 69 |
| | Practice | 70 |
| 6.5.4 | **The Indian Caste System** | |
| | Review | 71 |
| | Practice | 72 |
| 6.5.5 | **The Spread of Buddhism** | |
| | Review | 73 |
| | Practice | 74 |
| 6.5.6 | **The Maurya Empire** | |
| | Review | 75 |
| | Practice | 76 |
| 6.5.7 | **India's Legacy** | |
| | Review | 77 |
| | Practice | 78 |

6.6.1    **Origins of Chinese Civilization**

Review . . . . . . . . . . . . . . . . . . . . . . . . . . . . . . . . . . . . . . . . . . . . . . . . . .79

Practice. . . . . . . . . . . . . . . . . . . . . . . . . . . . . . . . . . . . . . . . . . . . . . . . .80

6.6.2    **The Geography of Ancient China**

Review . . . . . . . . . . . . . . . . . . . . . . . . . . . . . . . . . . . . . . . . . . . . . . . . . .81

Practice. . . . . . . . . . . . . . . . . . . . . . . . . . . . . . . . . . . . . . . . . . . . . . . . .82

6.6.3    **Confucianism and Taoism**

Review . . . . . . . . . . . . . . . . . . . . . . . . . . . . . . . . . . . . . . . . . . . . . . . . . .83

Practice. . . . . . . . . . . . . . . . . . . . . . . . . . . . . . . . . . . . . . . . . . . . . . . . .84

6.6.4    **Problems in China in the Time of Confucius**

Review . . . . . . . . . . . . . . . . . . . . . . . . . . . . . . . . . . . . . . . . . . . . . . . . . .85

Practice. . . . . . . . . . . . . . . . . . . . . . . . . . . . . . . . . . . . . . . . . . . . . . . . .86

6.6.5    **Achievements During the Qin Dynasty**

Review . . . . . . . . . . . . . . . . . . . . . . . . . . . . . . . . . . . . . . . . . . . . . . . . . .87

Practice. . . . . . . . . . . . . . . . . . . . . . . . . . . . . . . . . . . . . . . . . . . . . . . . .88

6.6.6    **The Han Dynasty**

Review . . . . . . . . . . . . . . . . . . . . . . . . . . . . . . . . . . . . . . . . . . . . . . . . . .89

Practice. . . . . . . . . . . . . . . . . . . . . . . . . . . . . . . . . . . . . . . . . . . . . . . . .90

6.6.7    **The Silk Roads**

Review . . . . . . . . . . . . . . . . . . . . . . . . . . . . . . . . . . . . . . . . . . . . . . . . . .91

Practice. . . . . . . . . . . . . . . . . . . . . . . . . . . . . . . . . . . . . . . . . . . . . . . . .92

6.6.8    **Buddhism Moves into China**

Review . . . . . . . . . . . . . . . . . . . . . . . . . . . . . . . . . . . . . . . . . . . . . . . . . .93

Practice. . . . . . . . . . . . . . . . . . . . . . . . . . . . . . . . . . . . . . . . . . . . . . . . .94

6.7.1    **Rise of the Roman Republic**

Review . . . . . . . . . . . . . . . . . . . . . . . . . . . . . . . . . . . . . . . . . . . . . . . . . .95

Practice. . . . . . . . . . . . . . . . . . . . . . . . . . . . . . . . . . . . . . . . . . . . . . . . .96

6.7.2    **Government of the Roman Republic**

Review . . . . . . . . . . . . . . . . . . . . . . . . . . . . . . . . . . . . . . . . . . . . . . . . . .97

Practice. . . . . . . . . . . . . . . . . . . . . . . . . . . . . . . . . . . . . . . . . . . . . . . . .98

6.7.3    **Growth of the Roman Empire**

Review . . . . . . . . . . . . . . . . . . . . . . . . . . . . . . . . . . . . . . . . . . . . . . . . . .99

Practice. . . . . . . . . . . . . . . . . . . . . . . . . . . . . . . . . . . . . . . . . . . . . . . .100

6.7.4    **Julius Caesar and Augustus**

Review . . . . . . . . . . . . . . . . . . . . . . . . . . . . . . . . . . . . . . . . . . . . . . . . .101

Practice. . . . . . . . . . . . . . . . . . . . . . . . . . . . . . . . . . . . . . . . . . . . . . . .102

6.7.5    **Judaism During the Roman Empire**

Review . . . . . . . . . . . . . . . . . . . . . . . . . . . . . . . . . . . . . . . . . . . . . . . . .103

Practice. . . . . . . . . . . . . . . . . . . . . . . . . . . . . . . . . . . . . . . . . . . . . . . .104

6.7.6    **Origins and Growth of Christianity**

Review . . . . . . . . . . . . . . . . . . . . . . . . . . . . . . . . . . . . . . . . . . . . . . . . .105

Practice. . . . . . . . . . . . . . . . . . . . . . . . . . . . . . . . . . . . . . . . . . . . . . . .106

6.7.7    **The Spread of Christianity**

Review . . . . . . . . . . . . . . . . . . . . . . . . . . . . . . . . . . . . . . . . . . . . . . . . .107

Practice. . . . . . . . . . . . . . . . . . . . . . . . . . . . . . . . . . . . . . . . . . . . . . . .108

6.7.8    **The Legacy of the Roman Empire**

Review . . . . . . . . . . . . . . . . . . . . . . . . . . . . . . . . . . . . . . . . . . . . . . . . .109

Practice. . . . . . . . . . . . . . . . . . . . . . . . . . . . . . . . . . . . . . . . . . . . . . . .110

## CA STANDARDS: REPORTING CLUSTER 2: LATE ANTIQUITY AND THE MIDDLE AGES

7.1    **The Roman Empire**

Review . . . . . . . . . . . . . . . . . . . . . . . . . . . . . . . . . . . . . . . . . . . . . . . . .111

Practice. . . . . . . . . . . . . . . . . . . . . . . . . . . . . . . . . . . . . . . . . . . . . . . .112

7.7    **Early Mesoamerican and Andean Civilizations**

Review . . . . . . . . . . . . . . . . . . . . . . . . . . . . . . . . . . . . . . . . . . . . . . . . .113

Practice. . . . . . . . . . . . . . . . . . . . . . . . . . . . . . . . . . . . . . . . . . . . . . . .114

# *How to Use This Book*

The *California Standards Enrichment Workbook* is yours to mark on, to write in, and to make your own. You can use it in class and take it home. The workbook will help you master social studies curriculum, point by point.

For each specific objective or goal in the Grade 6 California Content Standards, your book contains:

- a **Review** page, to summarize the most important content—the issues, ideas, and people behind important events.

- a **Practice** page, that asks you to recall, interpret, analyze, and apply the historical knowledge.

Complete the pages in the order your teacher assigns them. Your teacher will assign pages that match material in your social studies textbook.

You can use the **Quick Prep** section (pages 1–14) to scan important historic eras, leaders, data, and dates, and to look up and learn key terms. The Quick Prep section serves as a handy reference:

- As you work on Review and Practice pages, you can look up key ideas, dates, and definitions.

- The data can help you make inferences, make connections, or answer your own questions as they arise.

- Before a big test, you might use the Quick Prep to review with a peer, a tutor or family member, or on your own.

# Quick Prep

This Quick Prep section provides a handy reference to key facts on a variety of topics in world history.

## *Major Eras in World History*

The term era, or age, refers to a broad period of time characterized by a shared pattern of life. Eras and ages typically do not have exact starting and ending points. Because the historical development of different regions of the world is varied, no single listing of eras applies to all of world history. This chart applies primarily to Western civilization.

| Era and Dates | Description |
|---|---|
| **Stone Age** (2.5 million–3000 B.C.) | This long prehistoric period is often divided into two parts: the Old Stone Age, or Paleoli[...], and the New Stone Age, or Neolithic Age. The Paleolithic Age lasted from about 2.5 million t[...] B.C. During this time, hominids made and used stone tools and learned to control fire. The N[...] Age began about 8000 B.C., and ended about 3000 B.C., in some areas. In this period, people [...] to polish stone tools, make pottery, grow crops, and raise animals. The introduction of ag[...]e, a major turning point in human history, is called the Neolithic Revolution. |
| **Bronze Age** (3000–1200 B.C.) | People began using bronze, rather than stone and copper, to make tools and weapon[...]ronze Age began in Sumer about 3000 B.C., when Sumerian metalworkers found that they c[...]t together certain amounts of copper and tin to make bronze. The first civilizations em[...]uring the Bronze Age. |
| **Iron Age** (1500–1000 B.C. to the present day) | The use of iron to make tools and weapons became widespread. The Iron Age is the [...]hnological stage in the Stone-Bronze-Iron ages sequence. |
| **Classical Greece** (2000–300 B.C.) | Greek culture developed, rose to new heights, and spread to other lands. The Gree[...]tates established the first democratic governments. Greek scientists made advances in [...]atics, medicine, and other fields. The Greeks produced great works of drama, poetry, scu[...]architecture, and philosophy that still influence people today. |
| **Roman Empire** (500 B.C.–A.D. 500) | At its height, the Roman Empire united much of Europe, the north coast of Africa, [...]arge part of the Middle East. The Romans admired Greek art, literature, architecture, and sci[...]nd so they adopted and preserved much of Greek culture. The Romans also created their o[...]cy with outstanding achievements in engineering, architecture, the arts, and law. The R[...]spread Christianity throughout Europe, and their official language—Latin—gave rise to [...], Italian, Spanish, and other Romance languages. Western civilization has its roots in Gr[...]man culture. |
| **Middle Ages** (500–1200) | The West Roman Empire fell to Germanic conquerors who formed kingdoms out [...]mer Roman provinces. A new political and military system called feudalism became establis[...]Nobles were granted the use of lands that belonged to their king in exchange for their loyalty[...]ary service, and protection of the peasants who worked the land. Western Europe became divid[...]to feudal states. The Middle Ages was the time of castles and knights. |
| **Renaissance and Reformation** (1300–1600) | The Renaissance was a period of rebirth of learning and the arts based on a rev[...] of classical study. The study of Greek classics gave rise to an intellectual movement called humanis[...] which emphasized human potential and achievements rather than religious concerns. The works of [...]e Italian artists Leonardo da Vinci and Michelangelo and the English dramatist William Shakesp[...]re represent the cultural height of the Renaissance. The Reformation was a movement for religio[...] reform that led to the founding of Protestant churches. These churches rejected the authority of t[...] pope. The power of the Roman Catholic Church declined. |
| **Exploration and Colonization** (1400–1800) | The monarchs of Europe financed voyages around the world, motivated by the desire for riches and the hope of spreading Christianity. Seeking spices and converts, European explorers made long sea journeys to the East. Searching for a shorter sea route to Asia, Christopher Columbus landed in the Caribbean islands and opened up the New World to European colonization. The establishment of colonies and trading networks led to worldwide cultural exchange, but also to the devastation of Native American cultures in the New World, and the enslavement of millions of Africans. |
| **Revolution and Independence** (1700–1900) | Movements toward democracy and nationalism affected most countries in the Western world. These movements sparked the Revolutionary War in America, which resulted in the independence of the British colonies and the birth of the United States. They also sparked the ten-year French Revolution. Many Latin American nations fought colonial rule and gained their independence. In Europe, great empires fell and a system of nation-states became established. |

# Major Empires

| Name and Dates | Location | Achievements |
|---|---|---|
| **Akkadian** (c. 2350–2150 B.C.) | Mesopotamia | Became the world's first empire |
| **Alexandrian** (336–322 B.C.) | Greece, Persia, Egypt, northwest India | Spread Greek culture |
| **Assyrian** (c. 850–612 B.C.) | Southwest Asia, Egypt | Built one of the ancient world's largest libraries at Nineveh, the largest city of its day |
| **Athenian** (c. 480–420 B.C.) | Greece | Developed democratic principles and classical culture |
| **Austro-Hungarian** (late 1600s–1918) | Central Europe | Became known for its cultural life, especially its great composers |
| **Aztec** (1325–1521) | Mesoamerica | Built pyramids and developed a pictorial written language |
| **British** (1600s–1980s) | United Kingdom, Americas, Africa, Asia | Held one-fourth of the world's land and spread British culture to one-fourth of the world's people |
| **Byzantine** (395–1453) | Parts of southern and eastern Europe, northern Africa, and the Middle East | Preserved Greek culture, Roman customs, and Christianity and built the Hagia Sophia |
| **Egyptian** (2780–1075 B.C.) | Egypt, Nubia, parts of Syria and Palestine | Built magnificent palaces, temples, and pyramids |
| **Ghana** (800–1076) | West Africa | Became a center of the gold-salt trade |
| **Han** (201 B.C.–A.D. 220) | China | Established a centralized, bureaucratic government and unified Chinese culture |
| **Holy Roman** (962–1806) | Western and central Europe | Was the strongest state in Europe until about 1100 |
| **Inca** (1400–1532) | South America | Built a vast empire linked by an extensive road system |
| **Mali** (1200–1400) | West Africa | Became wealthy on the gold-salt trade and created an efficient government |
| **Maya** (250–900) | Mesoamerica | Built pyramids and developed the most advanced writing system in the ancient Americas |
| **Mongol** (about 1200–1294) | Europe, Asia | Created the largest unified land empire in history |
| **Mughal** (1526–1700s) | India | Built unique architecture, including the Taj Mahal |
| **Muslim** (661–1171) | Southwest Asia, North Africa | Spread scholarship and written culture |
| **Old Babylonian** (about 2000–1550 B.C.) | Mesopotamia | Compiled the Code of Hammurabi |
| **Ottoman** (about 1300–1922) | Turkey, North Africa, Southwest Asia, Southeast Europe | Became the world's most powerful empire in the 1500s and 1600s and built architectural masterpieces |
| **Persian** (about 550–330 B.C.) | Fertile Crescent, Anatolia, Egypt, India | Established a judicious, thoughtful, and tolerant government |
| **Roman** (27 B.C.–A.D. 476) | Europe, Mesopotamia, North Africa | Spread Greek and Roman culture, which became the basis of Western civilization |
| **Songhai** (1460s–1591) | West Africa | Gained control of trans-Saharan trade routes and built a thriving empire |

# Major Geographic Features

## United States and Canada

| Climate | | Vegetation | | Land Forms and Bodies of Water | |
|---|---|---|---|---|---|
| Arctic | Semi-arid | Tundra | Mediterranean | Great Lakes | Rocky Mountains |
| Sub-arctic | Sub-tropical | Coniferous forest | scrub | Gulf of Mexico | Mississippi River |
| Temperate | Tropical | Broadleaf forest | Semi-desert | Appalachian | |
| Arid | | Grassland | Desert | Mountains | |

## Latin America

| Climate | | Vegetation | | Land Forms and Bodies of Water | |
|---|---|---|---|---|---|
| Tropical | Temperate | Savannah | Tropical rainforest | Orinoco River | Sierra Madre |
| Sub-tropical | Arid | Semi-desert | Monsoon forest | Andes Mountains | Amazon River |
| Desert | Semi-arid | Desert | Broadleaf forest | | |
| | | Dry tropical scrub | | | |

## Europe, Russia, and the Independent Republics

| Climate | | Vegetation | | Land Forms and Bodies of Water | |
|---|---|---|---|---|---|
| Sub-arctic | Temperate | Tundra | Grassland | Baltic Sea | Volga River |
| Steppe | Mediterranean | Coniferous forest | Mediterranean | Mediterranean Sea | Alps Mountains |
| Tundra | Alpine | Broadleaf forest | scrub | North Sea | Pyrenees |
| Humid continental | | | | Lake Baikal | Mountains |
| | | | | Danube River | Ural Mountains |
| | | | | Rhine River | |

## North Africa and Southwest Asia

| Climate | | Vegetation | | Land Forms and Bodies of Water | |
|---|---|---|---|---|---|
| Desert | Temperate | Semi-desert | Monsoon forest | Red Sea | Sahara Desert |
| Sub-tropical | Arid | Desert | Dry tropical scrub | Persian Gulf | Nile River |
| Tropical | Semi-arid | | | Black Sea | Tigris River |
| Tropical monsoon | | | | Dead Sea | Euphrates River |

## Africa South of the Sahara

| Climate | | Vegetation | | Land Forms and Bodies of Water | |
|---|---|---|---|---|---|
| Tropical | Semi-arid | Savannah | Dry tropical scrub | Mount Kilimanjaro | Congo River |
| Sub-tropical | Desert | Semi-desert | Tropical rainforest | Kalahari Desert | Niger River |
| Arid | | Desert | Monsoon forest | Victoria Falls | Zambezi River |
| | | | | Nile River | |

## Southern Asia

| Climate | | Vegetation | | Land Forms and Bodies of Water | |
|---|---|---|---|---|---|
| Tropical | Sub-tropical | Monsoon forest | Sub-tropical forest | Himalayan | Mekong River |
| Monsoon | Moderate | Tropical rainforest | | Mountains | Arabian Sea |
| | | | | Mount Everest | South China Sea |
| | | | | Indus River | Bay of Bengal |
| | | | | Ganges River | Malay Archipelago |

## East Asia, Australia, and the Pacific Islands

| Climate | | Vegetation | | Land Forms and Bodies of Water | |
|---|---|---|---|---|---|
| Temperate | Sub-tropical | Savannah | Dry tropical scrub | Mount Fuji | Huang He |
| Arid | Tropical | Semi-desert | Tropical rainforest | Southern Alps | (Yellow River) |
| Semi-arid | | Desert | Monsoon forest | Gobi Desert | Chang Jiang |
| | | | | Great Barrier Reef | (Yangtze River) |

# Major Figures in Ancient History

| Name | Who the Person Was | What the Person Did |
|---|---|---|
| **Abraham** (2000 B.C.?) | Hebrew leader | Founded Judaism |
| **Akhenaton** (1375–1338 B.C.) | Egyptian pharaoh | Promoted worship of one god, Aten, the sun god |
| **Alexander the Great** (356–323 B.C.) | Macedonian king | Built an empire that included Greece, Persia, Egypt, and part of Central Asia |
| **Archimedes** (287–212 B.C.) | Greek mathematician, engineer, and physicist | Explained the law of the lever, invented the compound pulley and a device used to irrigate fields |
| **Aristophanes** (448?–380? B.C.) | Greek dramatist | Wrote comedies that made fun of politics, important people, and popular ideas |
| **Aristotle** (384–322 B.C.) | Greek philosopher | Summarized most knowledge up to his time and invented rules of logic that contributed to the modern scientific method |
| **Asoka** (200s B.C.) | Maurya king | Ruled peacefully, according to Buddhist teachings |
| **Augustus** (63 B.C.–A.D. 14) | Roman emperor | Ruled the Roman Empire at its peak |
| **Caesar, Julius** (100–44 B.C.) | Roman general and dictator | Expanded the Roman Empire |
| **Chandra Gupta II** (A.D. 355?–415) | Ruler of India | Ruled over a golden age in India—a time of great accomplishment |
| **Cicero** (106–43 B.C.) | Roman consul and orator | Opposed Julius Caesar's dictatorship; wrote philosophy and poetry |
| **Confucius** (551–479 B.C.) | Chinese scholar | Founded Confucianism |
| **Constantine the Great** (A.D. 285?–337) | Roman emperor | Ended the persecution of Christians and moved the capital of the Roman Empire to Byzantium, which was renamed Constantinople. |
| **David** (1000s B.C.) | King of the Israelites | Won control of Jerusalem in 1000 B.C. |
| **Diocletian** (A.D. 45–313) | Roman emperor | Introduced reforms in Rome's administration, army, and economy |
| **Euclid** (330?–270? B.C.) | Greek mathematician | Called the father of geometry for compiling the mathematics textbook *The Elements* |
| **Hammurabi** (?–1750 B.C.) | Babylonian king | Built the first great Babylonian Empire and compiled one of the first written collections of laws, the Code of Hammurabi |
| **Hannibal** (247–183 B.C.) | Carthaginian general | Led troops and elephants across the Alps to fight Rome in the Second Punic War |
| **Hatshepsut** (1400s B.C.) | Egyptian pharaoh | First woman to rule as pharaoh; declared herself ruler in 1472 B.C.; enriched Egypt by expanding trade |
| **Justinian** (A.D. 483–565) | Emperor of Eastern Roman Empire | Ruled with his wife Theodora from A.D. 527 to 565 and reconquered lost territories for the empire |
| **Khufu** (? –2560 B.C.) | Egyptian pharaoh | Ordered construction of the largest pyramid ever built |
| **Moses** (1300s B.C.?) | Israelite leader | Led the Jews out of Egypt and received the Ten Commandments |
| **Muhammad** (A.D. 570?–632) | Muslim prophet | Founded Islam |
| **Pacal** (A.D. 600s) | Mayan king | Ruler of the Mayan city-state called Palenque during its golden age |

| Name | Who the Person Was | What the Person Did |
|---|---|---|
| **Pericles** (494?–429 B.C.) | Greek statesman | Led Athens during its golden age, often called the Age of Pericles |
| **Plato** (427–347 B.C.) | Greek philosopher | Wrote *The Republic,* in which he described his ideal society |
| **Ramses** (1200s? B.C.) | Egyptian pharaoh | Ruled Egypt for 66 years, greatly expanding the Egyptian empire by conquering surrounding territories |
| **Shi Huangdi** (200s B.C.?) | Chinese ruler | Rose to power in 221 B.C. and unified and expanded China by ending internal battles and conquering rival states |
| **Siddhartha Gautama** (563?–483 B.C.) | Buddhist monk | Founded Buddhism |
| **Socrates** (469-399 B.C.) | Greek philosopher | Taught students to examine their beliefs and developed a question-and-answer method of teaching called the Socratic method. |
| **Thucydides** (471–400 B.C.) | Greek historian | Wrote a history of the Peloponnesian War, using documents and eyewitness accounts; set a standard for the writing of history |

# Major Events in Ancient History

| Time and Place | Event | Significance |
|---|---|---|
| 40,000 B.C.<br>Europe | Cro-Magnons appear. | Ancestors of modern humans |
| 8000 B.C.<br>Africa, Asia | Agriculture begins. | One of the great breakthroughs in human history, setting the stage for the development of civilizations |
| 3100 B.C.<br>Egypt | Upper and Lower Egypt unite. | The Kingdom of Egypt, ruled by pharaohs, began a 3,000-year period of unity and cultural continuity. |
| 3000 B.C.<br>Mesopotamia | Civilization emerges in Sumer. | One of the world's first civilizations |
| 2500 B.C.<br>Indus Valley | Planned cities arise. | Beginning of the Indus Valley civilization; many features of modern Indian culture can be traced to this early civilization. |
| 2350 B.C.<br>Mesopotamia | Sargon of Akkad builds an empire. | World's first empire, which extended from the Mediterranean coast in the west to present-day Iran in the east |
| 1700 B.C.<br>Asian steppes | Indo-Europeans begin migrations. | The Indo-Europeans moved into Europe, the Middle East, and India, spreading their languages and changing cultures. |
| 1766–1027 B.C.<br>China | Shang Dynasty begins. | The first Chinese civilization, which arose along the Huang He river |
| 1200 B.C.<br>Mexico | Olmec culture arises. | Oldest known civilization in the Americas |
| 850 B.C.<br>Assyria | Assyria builds an empire. | Using military force to conquer and rule, the Assyrians established an empire that included most of the old centers of power in Southwest Asia and Egypt. |
| 800 B.C.<br>Greece | Greek city-states arise. | Led to the development of several political systems, including democracy |
| 550 B.C.<br>Persia | Cyrus builds the Persian Empire. | Characterized by tolerance and wise government |
| 500 B.C.<br>Rome | Romans establish a republic. | Source of some of the most fundamental values and institutions of Western civilization |
| 461 B.C.<br>Greece | Age of Pericles begins. | Democratic principles and classical Greek culture flourished, leaving a legacy that endures to the present day. |
| 334 B.C.<br>Greece | Alexander begins to build an empire. | Conquered Persia and Egypt; extended his empire to the Indus River in India; resulted in a blending of Greek, Egyptian, and Eastern customs |
| 321 B.C.<br>India | Mauryan Empire is established. | United north India politically for the first time |
| 202 B.C.<br>China | Han Dynasty replaces Qin dynasty. | Expanded China's borders; developed a system of government that lasted for centuries |
| 27 B.C.<br>Rome | Octavian rules Roman Empire. | Took the title of Augustus and ruled the mightiest empire of the ancient world; began the *Pax Romana,* a 200-year period of peace and prosperity; Roman way of life spread throughout the empire. |
| A.D. 29<br>Jerusalem | Jesus is crucified. | Christianity spread throughout the Roman Empire. |
| A.D. 100<br>South America | Moche civilization emerges. | Built an advanced society in Peru |
| A.D. 100s<br>Africa | Bantu migrations begin. | Bantu speakers spread their language and culture throughout southern Africa. |
| A.D. 320<br>India | Gupta Empire begins. | A great flowering of Indian civilization, especially Hindu culture |
| A.D. 527<br>Constantinople | Justinian I becomes Byzantine emperor. | Recovered and ruled almost all the former territory of the Roman Empire; created a body of civil laws called Justinian's Code; built beautiful churches |

Copyright © McDougal Littell/Houghton Mifflin Company

| Time and Place | Event | Significance |
|---|---|---|
| 618<br>China | Tang dynasty begins. | Created a powerful empire, improved trade and agriculture, and restored the civil service bureaucracy |
| 600<br>Central America | Maya civilization thrives. | Built spectacular cities and developed the most advanced writing system in the ancient Americas |
| 800<br>North America | Anasazi civilization develops. | Ancestors of the Pueblo peoples |
| 800s–900s<br>West Africa | Empire of Ghana thrives. | Built its wealth on the trans-Saharan gold-salt trade |
| 814<br>Western Europe | Charlemagne unites much of Europe. | Established the Carolingian Empire |
| 960<br>China | Song Dynasty begins. | China became the most populous and advanced country in the world. |
| 1095<br>France | Pope Urban II issues call for First Crusade. | Stimulated trade, weakened the power of the pope and feudal nobles, and left a legacy of distrust between Christians and Muslims |
| 1192<br>Japan | Kamakura Shogunate begins. | First shogunate, which set the pattern for military dictators, called shoguns, to rule Japan until 1868 |
| 1200s<br>Mexico | Aztec civilization begins. | Built the greatest empire in Mesoamerica |
| 1200s<br>Peru | Inca Empire begins. | The largest empire in the Americas |
| 1209<br>Mongolia | Genghis Khan begins Mongol conquests. | Built the largest unified land empire in world history |
| 1215<br>England | King John agrees to Magna Carta. | The Magna Carta contributed to modern concepts of jury trials and legal rights. |
| 1235<br>Africa | Sundiata founds Mali Empire. | Became a powerful center of commerce and trade in West Africa |
| 1279<br>China | Kublai Khan conquers Song Dynasty. | Completed the conquest of China and encouraged trade; Chinese ideas then began to influence Western civilization. |
| 1300<br>Italy | Renaissance begins. | Revival of classical studies revolutionized art, literature, and society |

# *Major Religions*

| | Buddhism | Christianity | Hinduism | Islam | Judaism | Confucianism |
|---|---|---|---|---|---|---|
| | ☸ | ✝ | ॐ | ☪ | ✡ | ☯ |
| **Followers worldwide** (estimated 2003 figures) | 364 million | 2 billion | 828 million | 1.2 billion | 14.5 million | 6.3 million |
| **Name of god** | no god | God | Brahman | Allah | God | no god |
| **Founder** | the Buddha | Jesus | no founder | no founder but spread by Muhammad | Abraham | Confucius |
| **Holy book** | many sacred books, including the Dhammapada | Bible, including Old Testament and New Testament | many sacred texts, including the Upanishads | Qur'an | Hebrew Bible, including the Torah | *Analects* |
| **Clergy** | Buddhist monks | priests, ministers, monks, and nuns | Brahmin priests, monks, and gurus | no clergy but a scholar class, called the ulama, and imams, who may lead prayers | rabbis | no clergy |
| **Basic beliefs** | • Followers can achieve enlightenment by understanding the Four Noble Truths and by following the Noble Eightfold Path of right opinions, right desires, right speech, right action, right jobs, right effort, right concentration, and right meditation. | • There is only one God, who watches over and cares for his people.<br>• Jesus is the Son of God. He died to save humanity. His death and resurrection made eternal life possible for others. | • The soul never dies but is continually reborn until it becomes divinely enlightened.<br>• Persons achieve happiness and divine enlightenment after they free themselves from their earthly desires.<br>• Freedom from earthly desires comes from many lifetimes of worship, knowledge, and virtuous acts. | • Persons achieve salvation by following the Five Pillars of Islam and living a just life. The pillars are faith, prayer, charity, fasting, and pilgrimage to Mecca. | • There is only one God, who watches over and cares for his people.<br>• God loves and protects his people but also holds people accountable for their sins and shortcomings.<br>• Persons serve God by studying the Torah and living by its teachings. | • Social order, harmony, and good government should be based on strong family relationships.<br>• Respect for parents and elders is important to a well-ordered society.<br>• Education is important for the welfare of both the individual and society. |

**Source:** *World Almanac 2004*

Copyright © McDougal Littell/Houghton Mifflin Company

# Major Inventions in Ancient Times

Some dates are approximate, some are historically debated.

| Invention | Date | Significance |
|---|---|---|
| Controlled Fires | around 500,000 B.C. | • Facilitated cooking, early toolmaking, and better hunting |
| Flint and Stone Tools | around 300,000 B.C. | • Axes, grinding tools, knives |
| Irrigation | 5000 B.C. | • Brought water to crops; led to settled living and rise of early civilizations |
| Copper Working | 5000 B.C. | • First evidence of metal work, led to bronze work and later, iron work |
| Loom | 4000 B.C. | • Enabled people to weave cloth |
| Wheel | 3800 B.C. | • Easier and further transport of loads; became a part of vehicles and machines |
| Writing | 3500 B.C. | • Enabled record keeping, communication, shared history and scholarship |
| Plow | 3000 B.C. | • Made farming more productive |
| Glass Working | 2500 B.C. | • Primarily decorative; later used in containers, windows, and lenses |
| Musical Notation | 1300 B.C. | • Enabled shared musical culture |
| Iron Working | 1200 B.C. | • More effective tools and weapons |
| Aqueduct | 700 B.C. | • Brought water to cities, led to larger better-planned cities |
| Catapult | 400 B.C. | • Used for defense and war; allowed larger and further launch of weapons |
| Magnetic Compass | 300s B.C. | • Used for navigation; helped make longer sea voyages possible |
| Papermaking | 100 B.C. | • Spread written information and scholarship |
| Abacus | A.D.190 | • Allowed quick accurate calculation including square and cube roots |
| Algebra; Zero; Decimal Place | 500 | • Enabled abstract claculations and better recordkeeping |
| Windmill | 600 | • Power for grinding grain, pumping water; later used to generate electric power |
| Gunpowder | 800s | • Used in fireworks, bombs; influenced weapons development; later used in guns. |
| Magnifying Glass | 1250 | • Used for study of small matter and used in crafts |
| Gun / Cannon | 1260 | • Enabled weapons to be used at long range for better defense |

# Government and Economic Systems

| Government Systems | | |
|---|---|---|
| **System** | **Definition** | **Example** |
| aristocracy | Power is in the hands of a hereditary ruling class or nobility. | Medieval Europe |
| autocracy | A single person rules with unlimited power. Autocracy is also called dictatorship and despotism. | Pharaohs of ancient Egypt |
| democracy | Citizens hold political power either directly or through representatives. In a direct democracy, citizens directly make political decisions. In a representative democracy, the citizens rule through elected representatives. | ancient Athens (direct democracy) <br><br> United States since the 1700s (representative democracy) |
| federalism | Powers are divided among the federal, or national, government and a number of state governments. | United States since the 1700s |
| feudalism | A king allows nobles to use his land in exchange for their loyalty, military service, and protection of the people who live on the land. | Medieval Europe |
| military state | Military leaders rule, supported by the power of the armed forces. | Assyrian Empire |
| monarchy | A ruling family headed by a king or queen holds political power and may or may not share the power with citizen bodies. In an absolute monarchy, the ruling family has all the power. In a limited or constitutional monarchy, the ruler's power is limited by the constitution or laws of the nation. | reign of King Louis XIV of France (absolute monarchy) <br><br> United Kingdom (constitutional monarchy) |
| oligarchy | A few persons or a small group rule. | most ancient Greek city-states |
| parliamentary | Legislative and executive functions are combined in a legislature called a parliament. | United Kingdom since the 1200s |
| presidential | The chief officer is a president who is elected independently of the legislature. | United States since the 1700s |
| republic | Citizens elect representatives to rule on their behalf. | Roman Republic |
| theocracy | Religious leaders control the government, relying on religious law and consultation with religious scholars. In early theocracies, the ruler was considered divine. | Aztec Empire |
| totalitarianism | The government controls every aspect of public and private life and all opposition is suppressed. | Soviet Union under Joseph Stalin |

## Economic Systems

| System | Definition | Example |
|---|---|---|
| command | The production of goods and services is determined by a central government, which usually owns the means of production. Also called a planned economy. | former Soviet Union |
| communism | All means of production—land, mines, factories, railroads, and businesses—are owned by the people, private property does not exist, and all goods and services are shared equally. | former Soviet Union |
| free enterprise | Businesses are privately owned and operate competitively for profit, with minimal government interference. Also called capitalism. | United States |
| manorialism | A lord gives serfs land, shelter, and protection in exchange for work, and almost everything needed for daily life is produced on the manor, or lord's estate. | Medieval Europe |
| market | The production of goods and services is determined by the demand from consumers. Also called a demand economy. | United States |
| mixed | A combination of command and market economies is designed to provide goods and services so that all people will benefit. | present-day Israel |
| socialism | The means of production are owned by the public and operate for the welfare of all. | In many present-day countries, including Denmark and Sweden, the government owns some industries and operates them for the public good. |
| traditional | Goods and services are exchanged without the use of money; also called barter. | many ancient civilizations and tribal societies |

# Key Terms and Names

**Allah** God in the Islamic religion.

**astronomy** the study of planets, stars, and other celestial bodies.

**bubonic plague** a disease that struck western Eurasia in the mid-1300s, in an outbreak known as the Black Death.

**bureaucracy** a system of departments and agencies that carry out the work of a government.

**bushido** the code of conduct of samurai warriors, which required that they be generous, brave, and loyal.

**caliph** a ruler of the Muslim community, viewed as a successor of Muhammad.

**cartography** the skills and methods used in the making of maps.

**codex** a book of the type used by early Mesoamerican civilizations to record important historical events.

**cultural** diffusion the spread of ethnic ideas and customs to other areas of the world.

**daimyo** a Japanese lord with large landholdings and a private samurai army, who paid no taxes to the government.

**Diaspora** the scattering of Jewish people after they were forced out of Judea by the Romans in A.D. 70.

**dynastic cycle** the pattern of the rise and fall of dynasties.

**golden age** a period in which a society or culture is at its peak.

**griot** an official storyteller in an African civilization.

**Harappan civilization** an ancient Indian culture, dating back to 2500 B.C., that included the people of the entire Indus River region.

**Hindu-Arabic numerals** the numerals used in the United States and western Europe, which originated in India.

**Iberian Peninsula** the southwestern tip of Europe, where the modern nations of Spain and Portugal are located.

**imperial state** highly organized bureaucratic government in China developed during the Tang dynasty.

**independent judiciary** court system that operates without influence from other branches of the government.

**indulgence** a pardon for sin granted by the Roman Catholic Church.

**labor specialization** the doing of specific types of work by trained or knowledgeable workers.

**lord** a powerful landholding noble.

**manor** the estate of a feudal noble, usually including a fortified building or castle.

**mercantilism** an economic policy based on the idea that a nation's power depends on its wealth.

**Mesoamerica** a region that includes the southern part of Mexico and much of Central America.

**Ming Dynasty** the dynasty that assumed control of China in 1368 and restored China's imperial state.

**missionary** a person who travels to a foreign country in order to do religious work.

**Mongol Ascendancy** the period in which the Mongols controlled all of Central Asia, making overland trade and travel safe.

**monotheism** the belief that only one god exists.

**Muslim** a person who follows the religion of Islam, accepting Allah as the only God.

**natural law** a rule of conduct inferred from nature that governs people's actions in addition to or in place of laws handed down by human authority.

Copyright © McDougal Littell/Houghton Mifflin Company

**natural rights** the rights that all people are born with—such as the rights to life, liberty, and property according to the Enlightenment philosopher John Locke.

**nomad** a person who moves from place to place rather than settling permanently.

**parliament** a group of representatives with some powers of government.

**philosophy** an investigation of basic truths about the universe, based on logical reasoning.

**rationalism** the idea that people should use reason, or logical thought, to understand the world.

**samurai** a trained warrior of the Japanese aristocracy.

**savannah** a flat grassland, with few trees, in a tropical region.

**scholar-official** an educated person with a government position.

**scientific method** an approach to scientific investigation that involves making careful observations, forming and testing a hypothesis, and drawing a conclusion that confirms or modifies the hypothesis.

**senate** governing body of ancient Rome, made up of 300 members who advised Roman leaders.

**shogun** a Japanese military leader—one of a group that first came to power in 1192 and ruled on the emperor's behalf but usually in their own interests.

**Silk Roads** the ancient trade routes that connected Europe with China.

**Song Dynasty** period in China from 960 to 1279 in which trade and agriculture flourished.

**Sunnah** Muhammad's words and deeds, which serve Muslims as a guide for proper living.

**Tang Dynasty** period in China from 618 to the 900s during which time the imperial state was developed and China's unity was strengthened.

**trans-Saharan** across the Sahara.

**vegetation zone** a region that, because of its soil and climate, has distinctive types of plants.

**vernacular** a person's native language.

**wood-block printing** a printing system developed by the ancient Chinese, in which wood blocks were carved with enough characters to print entire pages.

**worldview** understanding and belief about the universe held by a group of people.

**Zen** a Japanese form of Buddhism, focusing on self-discipline, simplicity, and meditation.

## NAMES

**Abraham** according to the Bible, a shepherd from the city of Ur in Mesopotamia who became the father of the Hebrews.

**Aeneas** a hero of the Trojan War.

**Alexander the Great** king of Macedonia from 356 to 323 B.C., who conquered parts of Asia and Egypt, spreading Greek culture throughout his empire.

**Asoka** the greatest Maurya king, whose reign began in 269 B.C.

**Augustus** the first Roman emperor (originally named Octavian), who became emperor in 27 B.C.

**Caesar, Julius** a Roman general and politician (100–44 B.C.) who received great support from Rome's commoners and was given the right to rule for life in 44 B.C. He was assassinated the same year.

**Charlemagne (742–814)** King of the Franks (from 768) who conquered much of Europe and spread Christianity in the conquered regions.

**Constantine (285–337)** Roman emperor from A.D. 306 to 337, who ended the persecution of Christians and moved the capital of the empire to Byzantium (later known as Constantinople).

**David** the king of the Israelites who won control of Jerusalem in 1000 B.C.

**Hatshepsut** a female pharaoh of ancient Egypt, who initially ruled with her stepson but declared herself the only ruler in 1472 B.C.

**Murasaki Shikibu, Lady (978–1014)** Japanese writer whose work *The Tale of Genji* is considered one of the world's first novels.

**Piankhi** a king of Kush around 750 B.C., who gained control of almost all of Egypt, becoming pharaoh and uniting the two kingdoms.

**Shotoku, Prince (574–622)** Regent who ruled Japan from 593 to 622 and brought elements of Chinese culture—in particular, the Buddhist religion—to the country.

**Siddhartha Gautama** an Indian prince who founded Buddhism; also known as the Buddha.

Name _____  Date _____

**REVIEW**

CALIFORNIA CONTENT
STANDARD 6.1.2

# *The First Communities*

**SPECIFIC OBJECTIVE:** Identify the locations of human communities that populated the major regions of the world and describe how humans adapted to a variety of environments.

**Read the summary and map to answer questions on the next page.**

**River Valleys:** The earliest human settlements were based on agriculture. Many were in river valleys with fertile soil and easy access to water for irrigation and transportation. Early river-valley communities were located in the Huang He river valley in China, in the Indus river valley in India, along the Nile River in Africa, and between the Tigris and Euphrates rivers in Mesopotamia.

The farmers in Mesopotamia and in Egypt by the Nile were probably the first to use **irrigation**, setting up dikes and canals to water their crops. They adapted the environment so they did not have to depend on rainfall.

**Catul Huyak:** This settlement of about 5,000 people thrived around 8,000 years ago. Located near present-day Turkey, archeologists are still excavating the site.

**In the Americas:** Agricultural communities in the Americas started later than in other parts of the world, mostly in upland regions. Early farmers terraced the land to make flat areas where they could plant crops such as corn, beans, squash, and potatoes.

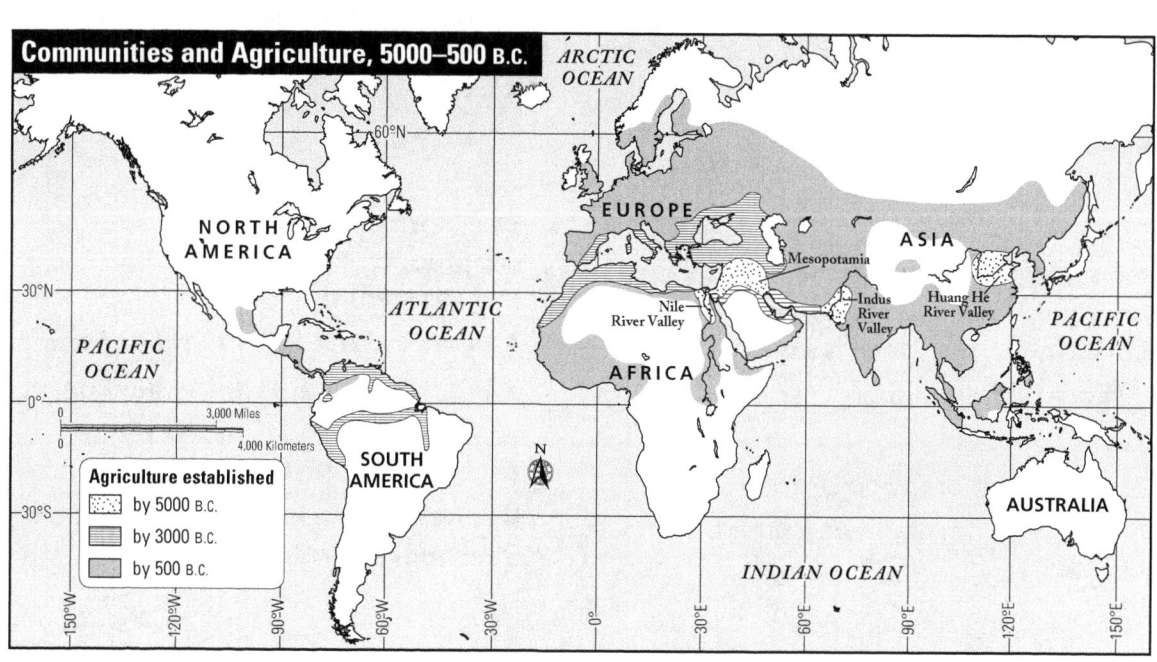

Name _____ Date _____

# The First Communities

**DIRECTIONS: Choose the letter of the *best* answer.**

**Use the map on page 17 to answer questions 1–3.**

**1** What is the relationship between the locations of early human settlements and agriculture?

- **A** There is no relationship between location and agricultural development.
- **B** Early communities arose where agriculture developed early.
- **C** Early communities arose where agriculture developed late.
- **D** Early communities were located in areas where agriculture had not yet developed.

**2** *Two* areas of the world where agriculture was late to develop were

- **A** South America and Africa.
- **B** Africa and Australia.
- **C** Australia and North America
- **D** Asia and Africa.

**3** Compared to other parts of the world, the development of agriculture in the Americas was

- **A** more widespread.
- **B** much earlier.
- **C** later, but more widespread.
- **D** later, and not very widespread.

**4** *One* early example of humans adapting their environment was

- **A** burning down forests to make space for communities.
- **B** creating reservoirs for human drinking.
- **C** building complex systems of highways through mountains.
- **D** learning to irrigate their land so there would be water during dry spells.

**5** Early human communities often grew up in river valleys because

- **A** the soil was fertile and there was water for irrigation and travel.
- **B** the temperatures were warmer in those areas.
- **C** people used the river to travel to new places for settlement.
- **D** that was where their leaders said they must live.

**6** Early farmers in the Americas adapted, or changed, the environment by

- **A** clearing the forests and swamps.
- **B** making terraces in the land on which to plant their crops.
- **C** being the first to use irrigation.
- **D** melting glaciers and warming air temperatures.

# *Learning to Use the Environment*

**SPECIFIC OBJECTIVE:** Discuss the climatic changes and human modifications of the physical environment that gave rise to the domestication of plants and animals and new sources of clothing and shelter.

**Read the summary to answer questions on the next page.**

**The End of the Ice Age:** Scientists say the Earth was once much colder than it is today. Many places were covered by great sheets of ice. Then, about 10,000 years ago, Earth gradually became warmer, and the ice began to melt. Many animals could not survive in the warmer climate. As glaciers retreated and temperatures rose, groups of people moved into warmer parts of the world.

**The Agricultural Revolution:** Agriculture began around 8000 B.C. when people first realized they could plant seeds and grow crops, rather than gathering them in the wild. People **domesticated**, or tamed, plants, and learned how to raise them themselves. People also domesticated wild animals (including sheep, pigs, and goats), using them as a reliable source of meat, milk, and skins. Some animals were raised for work. Dogs helped with hunting and protected early humans; horses and donkeys plowed and carried heavy loads.

**The Earliest Communities:** Once people had a reliable source of food, they built more permanent settlements. Farming villages replaced the temporary campsites of hunters and gatherers. People invented new tools that made farming easier. With these new tools, they could produce a **surplus**, or more food than they needed. Once people produced a surplus of food, they realized that some people did not need to farm. They could **specialize**, making a living by weaving cloth or making pottery. People who earn their living at a craft are called artisans.

**The Rise of Government:** As the number of artisans grew, so did the size of villages. Some villages became towns. With the growth of towns came changes. Trade between farmers and artisans increased. At the same time, towns needed leaders to defend communities from attack and settle arguments. Government was becoming organized. Social classes also arose, with the town leader or priest often at the top of society. Communities were beginning to resemble what they are today.

**PRACTICE**

CALIFORNIA CONTENT
STANDARD 6.1.3

*Learning to Use the Environment*

**DIRECTIONS: Choose the letter of the *best* answer.**

**1** Which statement *best* describes what happened at the end of the last Ice Age, about 10,000 years ago?

  **A** There were fewer people and more wild animals.

  **B** Many animals died off, and people moved to warmer parts of the world.

  **C** Glaciers covered areas of the world once used for agriculture.

  **D** New types of nutritious plants began to grow in some places.

**2** Agriculture began around 8000 B.C. when people realized that

  **A** they could grow crops, rather than gather them.

  **B** they could produce a surplus and become artisans.

  **C** government leaders were needed to protect towns from danger.

  **D** trading with other towns was now possible.

**3** Domestication of animals meant that humans

  **A** had learned to appreciate the benefits of owning pets.

  **B** did not have to work hard anymore.

  **C** could raise animals, rather than hunt them for food.

  **D** went from being vegetarians to eating meats and vegetables.

**4** How did the development of new tools affect agricultural production?

  **A** Farmers could now grow anything in any climate.

  **B** Farming became more expensive because of the cost of tools.

  **C** New tools increased agricultural output and led to surpluses.

  **D** More education was required to become a farmer.

**5** How did agricultural surpluses lead to specialization and increased trade?

  **A** Potters and weavers used tools to make their goods.

  **B** Traders were not interested in agricultural products.

  **C** With better diets, more people could become artisans.

  **D** Surpluses meant not everyone had to farm all the time.

**6** Why was government needed as small villages grew into larger towns?

  **A** Leaders were needed to make sure farmers produced a surplus.

  **B** There was no longer specialization, so someone was needed to decide how each person made a living.

  **C** Most people did as they pleased; a ruler was needed to act as a dictator.

  **D** Towns needed leaders to settle arguments and defend the towns from outside attack.

Name _____ Date _____

**CALIFORNIA CONTENT
STANDARD 6.2.1**

*Early River Civilizations*

**SPECIFIC OBJECTIVE:** Locate and describe the major river systems and discuss the physical settings that supported permanent settlement and early civilizations.

**Read the summary to answer questions on the next page.**

## Mesopotamia, Land Between the Rivers

- **The Tigris-Euphrates:** About 7,000 years ago, farming villages began in the Tigris-Euphrates river valley in Southwest Asia. The rivers flooded in spring, leaving behind rich soil. In summer, the area was dry.

- **Irrigation:** Flooding of the rivers was unpredictable. Around 6000 B.C., farmers began irrigation, or bringing water to their crops.

- **City-States:** In time, irrigation allowed farmers to grow surplus crops. With a surplus of food, people began to specialize. Towns turned into city-states, each ruled by its own leader and armies.

- **Sumer:** By about 3300 B.C., one of the world's first civilizations arose in Sumer, the southern part of Mesopotamia (present-day Iraq).

## Egypt

- **The Nile River:** People have lived in the Nile River Valley for thousands of years. Beyond it lies the dry, extremely hot, desert.

- **Flooding:** Compared to the unpredictable Tigris River, the Nile overflowed its banks regularly. The Egyptians worshiped the Nile as a god who gave them life.

- **United Country:** The Nile allowed people to travel north to south. It also protected them from invaders. Unlike Sumer, Egypt was not divided. Beginning around 3000 B.C., Egypt was unified.

## China

- **Huang He:** China's first farmers lived along the Huang He River in northern China about 5,000 years ago, when Chinese civilization began. Over many hundreds of years, farming spread south, mainly to other river valleys.

- **The Countryside:** Villagers in the north grew wheat and mullet. In the south, they grew rice. Many fields were built on step-like fields known as terraces.

## India

- **The Indus River** stretches through the Himalayas to the north of India. Indian civilization arose along this river about 5,000 years ago.

- **Settlements:** Along the river, there were many villages where people farmed. In the cities, workers earned a living in a variety of ways.

**PRACTICE**

CALIFORNIA CONTENT
STANDARD 6.2.1

*Early River Civilizations*

**DIRECTIONS: Choose the letter of the *best* answer.**

**1** Mesopotamia was located in which region?

**A** North Africa

**B** Southern Africa

**C** Southwest Asia

**D** Northeast Asia

**2** The first civilization that emerged in Mesopotamia, around 3300 B.C., was

**A** in Sumer, in southern Mesopotamia.

**B** in Kush, in the center of Mesopotamia.

**C** in Egypt, by the Nile.

**D** in Babylon, in the north of Mesopotamia.

**3** *One* factor that made farming easier in ancient Egypt than in Mesopotamia was that

**A** Egyptians invented irrigation earlier than the Mesopotamians.

**B** there were fewer trees that needed to be uprooted.

**C** the Nile flooded predictably, unlike the Tigris and Euphrates.

**D** Egypt, unlike Mesopotamia, was in a river floodplain.

**4** Which region came to be divided into city-states?

**A** the land along the Nile

**B** the Huang He river valley

**C** the land between the Tigris and Euphrates rivers

**D** the Indus river valley

**5** In which civilization did farmers build terraces?

**A** Mesopotamia

**B** China

**C** Egypt

**D** India

**REVIEW**

**CALIFORNIA CONTENT
STANDARD 6.2.2**

*Early Centers of Culture*

**SPECIFIC OBJECTIVE:** Trace the development of agricultural techniques that permitted the production of economic surplus and the emergence of cities as centers of culture and power.

**Read the summary to answer questions on the next page.**

### Sumer, a Center of Culture and Power

Ancient Sumerians were the first group of people to build cities. Most scholars believe that cities are just one of the traits that make a group of people civilized. What else marked the Sumerians as the first group to build a **civilization**?

**Cities:** By 3000 B.C., the Sumerians had about a dozen cities. Population alone does not make a village into a city. One of the most important differences between a city and a village is that a city is a center of trade for a larger area.

**Specialized workers:** In Sumer, for the first time, farmers were able to raise enough food to have a **surplus,** or more than they needed. This was due in part to the use of **irrigation,** which allowed farmers to bring water to their fields in the summer when fields were dry. Sumerians could trade their extra food for goods produced by **artisans,** skilled workers who make goods by hand. A surplus of food freed some people to do specialized jobs.

**Writing:** Another trait of civilization is writing. Scholars call Sumerian writing **cuneiform**. Sumerians invented writing as a necessity. For example, merchants needed accounts of debts and payments.

**Advanced technology:** The Sumerians were skilled in science and technology. They built irrigation ditches and invented the wheel, the plow, and the sailboat. Using the plow and irrigation, farmers could produce the food surplus that Sumer's cities needed. Another technology in Sumer was the ability to work with metal. After 2500 B.C., metalworkers in Sumer were able to make bronze spearheads by the thousands. Beginning around 2800 B.C., this period is called the **Bronze Age.**

**Complex institutions:** Government is an example of a complex institution. Sumerians were the first people to set up formal governments with officials and laws. Organized religion is another type of institution. Sumerian city-states had a formal religion that included great temples.

**PRACTICE**

CALIFORNIA CONTENT
STANDARD 6.2.2

*Early Centers of Culture*

**DIRECTIONS: Choose the letter of the *best* answer.**

**1** What makes a city distinct and different from a village?

  **A** Cities have more people than villages.

  **B** Cities unite large bands of hunters and gatherers.

  **C** Unlike a village, a city is a center of trade for a larger area.

  **D** In cities, people worship more powerful gods than in rural areas.

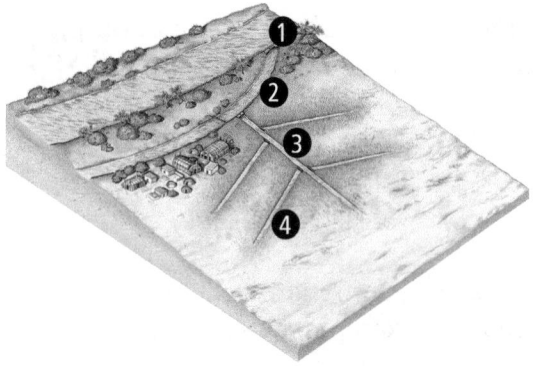

**2** What is the function of the part of an irrigation system shown by number 4 on the diagram?

  **A** stop and start water flow with a gate

  **B** capture naturally flowing water when it floods

  **C** carry water from underground wells

  **D** bring water across distances to fields of crops

**3** In addition to cities, what are *four* other traits that define a civilization?

  **A** irrigation ditches; a belief in local gods; artisans; farming

  **B** local customs; gathering wild plants; language; making spears from pointed rocks

  **C** specialized workers; writing; advanced technology; complex institutions

  **D** the worship of local gods; hunting; living close to the land; plows

**4** A surplus of food in Ancient Sumer meant that some people could be

  **A** herders.

  **B** hunters and gatherers.

  **C** specialized workers.

  **D** farmers.

**5** In addition to irrigation, what other technological advance led to the production of a surplus of food?

  **A** the wheel

  **B** the plow

  **C** mathematics

  **D** cuneiform

REVIEW

CALIFORNIA CONTENT
STANDARD 6.2.3

## The Role of Religion in Ancient Culture

**SPECIFIC OBJECTIVE:** Understand the relationship between religion and the social and political order in Mesopotamia and Egypt.

**Read the summary to answer questions on the next page.**

## Mesopotamia

- **Society:** Each city and the surrounding countryside was a **city-state.** Society was divided into groups. At the top were priests and kings. Wealthy merchants ranked second. Most Sumerians worked with their hands in fields and workshops. At the lowest level were enslaved people.

- **Many gods:** The Sumerians were **polytheists,** or believers in many gods. They worshiped roughly 3,000 gods.

- **Priests:** Sumer's earliest government was controlled by priests who lived within the high walls of the **ziggurat,** or temple.

- **Kings:** During a war, priests did not lead the city. Instead, the men of the city chose a fighter to lead the city's soldiers temporarily. As wars became more frequent, the commander gradually became a full-time king. After 3000 B.C., every Sumerian city-state was ruled both by powerful priests and a king.

## Egypt

- **Society:** Ancient Egypt was organized much like a pyramid. The king and a few powerful families were at the top. In the middle were merchants and artisans. Most Egyptians were near the bottom. Enslaved people formed the lowest level.

- **Many gods:** Egyptians were also polytheists. Their main god was Ra, the sun god, source of all life. Osiris, the god of the Nile, was much loved. Horus shared his powers with the pharaoh.

- **Pharaohs:** The kings of ancient Egypt were called **pharaohs,** which means "great house." In Mesopotamia, kings were representatives of the gods. In ancient Egypt, pharaohs were gods.

- **Priests:** After the pharaoh, Egyptian priests were the most important people in society. Priests took care of the temples, were in charge of ceremonies, and spoke on behalf of the gods.

- **Pyramids:** Ancient Egyptians believed that their pharaohs ruled even after death. Within a pyramid's burial chamber were all the riches a pharaoh would need for life in the next world. Egyptians mummified, or preserved, the pharaoh's body so he could have it for the afterlife. Unlike Sumerians, Egyptians had a positive worldview and believed in a pleasant life after death.

**PRACTICE**

CALIFORNIA CONTENT
STANDARD 6.2.3

# The Role of Religion in Ancient Culture

---

**DIRECTIONS: Choose the letter of the *best* answer.**

**1** *One* thing early Egyptian and Mesopotamian cultures had in common was

  **A** mummies.

  **B** polytheism.

  **C** ziggurats.

  **D** optimism.

**2** What was the relationship between the Sumerian and Egyptian views of life and the afterlife?

  **A** Both cultures were positive about life and negative about the afterlife.

  **B** Both cultures were negative about life but positive about the afterlife

  **C** Egyptians had the more positive view about life and afterlife.

  **D** Sumerians had the more positive view about life and afterlife.

**3** In ancient Egypt, the pharaoh was both a king and

  **A** a merchant.

  **B** an artisan.

  **C** a priest.

  **D** a god.

**4** In ancient Egypt, the purpose of mummifying the pharaoh's body was to

  **A** make the pharaoh into a priest.

  **B** preserve the pharaoh's body for the afterlife.

  **C** make sure the bodies of the pharaohs did not spread disease.

  **D** make the pharaoh into a god.

**5** In ancient Sumerian city-states, the Ziggurat was the

  **A** tomb of the pharaoh.

  **B** form of Sumerian writing.

  **C** center of the pharaoh's palace.

  **D** center of religious and cultural life.

**6** Egyptian and Sumerian government were similar in

  **A** basing law on religion.

  **B** separation of church and state.

  **C** passing laws by democratic process.

  **D** leadership by a god-king.

**REVIEW**

CALIFORNIA CONTENT
STANDARD 6.2.4

# *Hammurabi's Code*

**SPECIFIC OBJECTIVE:** Know the significance of Hammurabi's Code.

**Read the summary to answer questions on the next page.**

## The Babylonians

Around 2000 B.C., new groups of people moved into Southwest Asia. The first group of conquerors came from Babylon, a city upstream from Sumer. The major achievement of the Babylonians was a code of laws. It helped unite the large Babylonian empire.

## Hammurabi

- Ruled the Babylonian empire from 1792 to 1750 B.C.
- Expanded the empire across Mesopotamia and other parts of Southwest Asia
- Adapted civilization of Sumerians, including ziggurats, cuneiform (writing), and irrigation
- Most famous for "code of laws" (1750 B.C.)

## Code of Laws

- Chiseled by a scribe on an eight-foot slab of black stone outside a temple
- Written in cuneiform, wedge-shaped form of writing first used by Sumerians
- Contained 282 laws covering business, property, and personal conduct
- Chose the best or fairest laws among city-states he ruled
- Eliminated disagreements and contradictions in laws, making a "code" rather than a list of laws
- Hammurabi's idea of justice: an eye for an eye, a tooth for a tooth, a life for a life
- Established harsh but consistent punishments
- Identified acts of wrongdoing and gave rights to citizens
- Gave some rights to women and children
- Doled out different punishments for different social classes

## The Legacy

- Instituted tradition of society being governed by rule of law
- Established role of government in protecting the people
- Replaced personal revenge with codified system of laws
- Recorded in writing in public for everyone to see and obey
- Small crime did not lead to great punishment

Name _____  Date _____

# Hammurabi's Code

**DIRECTIONS: Choose the letter of the *best* answer.**

**1** From about 1792–1750 B.C., which group of people ruled much of Southwest Asia?

  **A** the Sumerians

  **B** the Egyptians

  **C** the Babylonians

  **D** the Mesopotamians

**2** How did Hammurabi's "code" of laws differ from a "list" of laws?

  **A** It dictated the punishment for one person poking out the eye of another.

  **B** He chose the laws that seemed best to him and eliminated contradictions.

  **C** It gave different punishment to different social classes.

  **D** It gave some rights to women and children.

**3** In Hammurabi's code, an eye for an eye, a tooth for a tooth, and a life for a life meant that

  **A** the punishment had to fit the crime.

  **B** a person could lose an eye for stealing a bag of grain.

  **C** the code was harsh and unfair.

  **D** the laws only covered crimes involving bodily harm.

**4** Why was it important that Hammurabi had his code written down on a slab of stone outside a temple?

  **A** It was important that temple priests follow the laws.

  **B** Paper had not yet been invented, so carving was the only way to write.

  **C** Anyone could change the laws by adding to or rewriting them.

  **D** The laws were public so that people would know and follow them.

**5** In order to gather laws for his code, Hammurabi

  **A** analyzed the laws of his subjects and took the best ones.

  **B** consulted astronomers.

  **C** thought for a long time about what was fair.

  **D** compiled several codes written by the Sumerians.

**REVIEW**

CALIFORNIA CONTENT
STANDARD 6.2.5

# Egyptian Art and Architecture

**SPECIFIC OBJECTIVE:** Discuss the main features of Egyptian art and architecture.

**Read the summary to answer questions on the next page.**

One feature of Egyptian civilization that supported art and architecture was the belief in life after death. Much information about life in ancient Egypt comes from sacred texts and wall paintings on the temples and tombs of pharaohs and wealthy nobles.

## Great Age of Pyramid Building: 2660–2180 B.C.

- **Purpose:** built as tombs for pharaohs
- **Contents:** filled with treasure for use of pharaoh in afterlife
- **Remains:** 80 pyramids still stand in Egyptian desert; robbed of treasures

## The Great Pyramid

- **Where:** built at Giza; today part of Greater Cairo
- **When:** 2550 B.C. by the pharaoh, Khufu
- **Statistics:** covered 13 acres; as tall as a skyscraper 40 stories high; each side 760 feet long; core built from 2.3 million blocks of stone; tallest structure on earth for more than 4,300 years
- **Contained:** 125-foot ship to transport pharaoh's soul; great treasures
- **Builders:** nearly 20 years to build; probably built by farmers during flood season when land could not be worked
- **Method:** built before Egyptians used wheel; workers probably made huge mud-brick ramps beside pyramid; splashed water over ramp to make slippery

## Astronomy and Geometry

- **Priest-Astronomers:** used measurements from stars to align pyramids and temples with the four directions of the compass
- **Geometric Shapes:** geometry considered sacred; used in temples and monuments

## Art

- **Purpose:** to glorify both the gods and the dead
- **Technique:** Strict rules governed how to paint people; paintings of the face were always in profile; paintings of the body showed the front.
- **Large Works:** art created for temples, attached to the royal pyramids
- **Jewelry:** made from gold and precious stones such as turquoise and lapis lazuli

**PRACTICE**

CALIFORNIA CONTENT
STANDARD 6.2.5

# Egyptian Art and Architecture

**DIRECTIONS: Choose the letter of the *best* answer.**

**1** Much of Ancient Egyptian art and architecture was connected to

  **A** a love of music.

  **B** hieroglyphics.

  **C** a belief in life after death.

  **D** constant warfare.

**2** *One* unique aspect of ancient Egyptian paintings is that faces are always shown in

  **A** white.

  **B** profile.

  **C** hieroglyphics.

  **D** three dimensions.

**3** What world record did the Great Pyramid hold for more than 4,300 years?

  **A** It was the oldest known pyramid in the world.

  **B** It was the first step pyramid.

  **C** It had taken longer to build than any other structure.

  **D** It was the tallest structure on earth.

**4** How did priests use astronomy to build the pyramids?

  **A** to align pyramids with directions of the compass

  **B** to measure the bases to exact lengths

  **C** to figure out when to build them

  **D** to be sure certain stars could be viewed from the windows

**5** Which artifact has been *most* useful to historians learning about life in ancient Egypt?

  **A** a codified system of Egyptian laws found in every pyramid

  **B** texts of ancient Egyptian astrologers

  **C** diaries and journals kept by the women of wealthy families

  **D** texts and paintings found on the walls of temples and tombs

**6** It is *likely* that the Great Pyramid at Giza was built by

  **A** thousands of enslaved people.

  **B** Egyptian farmers during the flood season.

  **C** builders and artists hired by the pharaohs.

  **D** volunteers from the Egyptian army.

Name _____    Date _____

# Egyptian Trade in the Ancient World

**SPECIFIC OBJECTIVE:** Describe the role of Egyptian trade in the eastern Mediterranean and Nile valley.

**Read the summary to answer questions on the next page.**

## Trade in Ancient Egypt

The Nile River was important to ancient Egyptians. They used the Nile to travel from north to south. From the mouth of the Nile, they traveled to other countries around the Mediterranean Sea. Egypt traded with Nubia, Crete, Cyprus, Greece, Kush, and Palestine. The Egyptians did not use money, so all their trade was based on barter, or trading one thing for another.

## Queen Hatshepsut and Trade

During the period of the New Kingdom (1570–1075 B.C.), Queen Hatshepsut ruled boldly for 22 years. Unlike most New Kingdom rulers, she was better known for encouraging trade than waging war. Hatshepsut expanded Egypt's trade boundaries. She sent an expedition across the eastern desert to the Red Sea. Ships sailed south on the Red Sea to an African country called Punt. From Punt, traders returned with rare herbs, spices, scented woods, live monkeys, and potted trees.

## Ramses II

Another pharaoh, Ramses II (1279–1213 B.C.), later expanded the Egyptian empire and Egyptian trade by marrying two daughters of a Hittite king. (Ramses II had eight wives.) The Hittites were fierce warriors who had built a large empire in Mesopotamia, Syria, and Palestine. They were also famous traders who carried the legacy of ancient Sumer wherever they went.

| What Egypt Traded | What Egypt Traded For |
|---|---|
| copper | horses |
| gold | cattle |
| lapus lazuli | monkeys |
| turquoise | ivory |
| papyrus sheets | incense |
| linen | silver |
| wheat | cedar logs |
| barley | leopard skins |
| | spices |

**PRACTICE**

CALIFORNIA CONTENT
STANDARD 6.2.6

# Egyptian Trade in the Ancient World

**DIRECTIONS: Choose the letter of the *best* answer.**

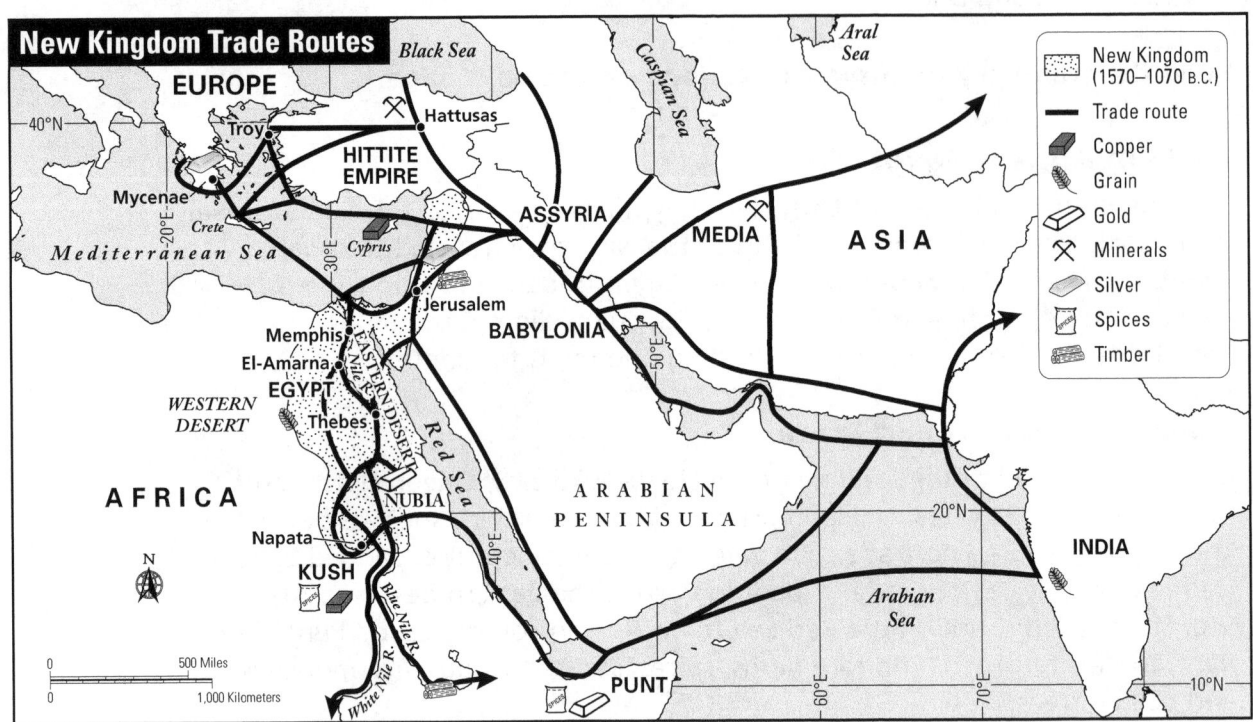

**New Kingdom Trade Routes**

Legend: New Kingdom (1570–1070 B.C.), Trade route, Copper, Grain, Gold, Minerals, Silver, Spices, Timber

**Use the map to answer questions 1 and 2.**

**1** To the east, Egyptian trade routes went as far as

　　**A** Greece.

　　**B** Babylonia.

　　**C** the Hittite Empire.

　　**D** India.

**2** How was gold transported from Nubia to Egypt?

　　**A** across the Mediterranean Sea.

　　**B** by land routes across the eastern desert.

　　**C** across the Arabian Sea.

　　**D** by sailing north on the Nile River.

**3** What was Egypt's *greatest* asset in trading?

　　**A** gold

　　**B** the Nile

　　**C** spices

　　**D** Ramses II

**4** Egyptians often traded their gold, precious stones, and grain for

　　**A** animals.

　　**B** copper.

　　**C** lapis lazuli.

　　**D** linen.

**REVIEW**

# *Hatshepsut and Ramses*

**SPECIFIC OBJECTIVE:** Understand the significance of Queen Hatshepsut and Ramses the Great.

**Read the summary to answer questions on the next page.**

## Queen Hatshepsut

- **Becoming Pharaoh:** first female pharaoh; declared herself pharaoh around 1478 B.C., after the death of her young husband and while her stepson was a child; often wore a man's kilt and attached the pharaoh's long braided ceremonial beard to her chin

- **Deeds and Accomplishments:**
  —more of a trader than a warrior pharaoh

  —made Egypt richer by expanding trade with other countries

  —biggest expedition crossed the eastern desert and sailed south on the Red Sea to Punt

  —proclaimed glory with an obelisk, a tall four-sided tower with a pyramid-shaped top

- **End of Reign:** No one knows how she died; may have been murdered by her stepson, the impatient-to-rule Thutmose III, who succeeded her and tried to destroy all records of her reign.

## Ramses II

- **Beginnings:** came to throne in 1279 B.C.; known as Ramses the Great
- **Reign:** ruled for 66 years—a stable period in Egyptian history and one of the longest reigns in history; had many wives and over 100 children; built the Abu Simbel temple, which was guarded by four 66-foot idealized statues of himself; last of Egypt's pharaohs
- **Accomplishments:**
  —expanded the Egyptian empire south to Nubia and north to eastern rim of Mediterranean

  —used war to make Egypt more powerful

  —declared war on the fierce Hittites and negotiated the first known peace treaty

  —married two of the Hittite king's daughters in order to sustain peace

  —one of greatest builders of New Kingdom

**PRACTICE**

**CALIFORNIA CONTENT
STANDARD 6.2.7**

## *Hatshepsut and Ramses*

**DIRECTIONS: Choose the letter of the *best* answer.**

**1** Hatshepsut of ancient Egypt was famous for being the

   **A** most important wife of Ramses.

   **B** first female pharaoh.

   **C** mother of Tutankhamen.

   **D** beloved wife of Akhenaton.

**2** Ramses II is unique in history as a pharaoh because of

   **A** his great strength.

   **B** the fact that he never married.

   **C** the length of his reign.

   **D** his peaceful nature.

**3** What followed from Ramses's war with the Hittites?

   **A** the defeat of Egypt

   **B** a new Egyptian-Hittite kingdom

   **C** the first expedition to Punt

   **D** the first known peace treaty

**4** The monument Hatshepsut built for herself was

   **A** an obelisk.

   **B** the Great Pyramid.

   **C** the Abu Simbel temple.

   **D** the  Sphinx.

**5** Queen Hatshepsut contributed to Egyptian history by

   **A** marrying a Hittite king.

   **B** expanding trade.

   **C** increasing the size of the empire.

   **D** negotiating a peace treaty.

**6** Ramses the Great contributed to Egyptian history by

   **A** expanding the empire.

   **B** conquering the Hittites and enslaving their women.

   **C** sending traders to Punt.

   **D** building the Pyramid at Giza.

**REVIEW**

CALIFORNIA CONTENT
STANDARD 6.2.8

## *Ancient Kush*

**SPECIFIC OBJECTIVE:** Identify the location of the Kush civilization and describe its political, commercial, and cultural relations with Egypt.

**Read the summary to answer questions on the next page.**

**Nubia and Kush**  The ancient Egyptians lived on the lower, or northern, end of the Nile. South of Egypt was another civilization that arose around 700 B.C. The region was Nubia, and its kingdom was called Kush.

### Nubia

- **Location:** geographic region in Africa; south of Egypt in the middle of the Nile Valley; climate moister than Egypt; not as dependent on the Nile
- **Relationship with Egypt:** controlled by Egypt between 2000 and 1000 B.C.; Nubian nobles adopted Egyptian ways of dress, art, architecture, writing; Nubia also influenced Egypt; may have influenced Egyptians to have one king or pharaoh; rich cultural exchanges between Nubia and Egypt

### Rise of Kush

- As Egypt declined, a Nubian kingdom named Kush came to power in 700s B.C. The Kushite king, Piankhi, attacked the city of Memphis in Egypt. Thirty-six years later, Kush had control of Egypt.

#### Napata Period

- **Piankhi:** united Kush and Egypt in 751 B.C.; became pharaoh, starting Egypt's 25th Dynasty; ruled from Napata, capital of Kush
- **Trade:** became trading center for spread of Egyptian goods and ways of life to Kush's other trading partners in Africa and beyond
- **Location:** head of a road used to move goods around the Nile's cataracts; good location
- **Threat of Assyrians:** 671 B.C., Assyrians threatened Kush; fierce fighters; carried iron weapons stronger than Kushite bronze; first cavalry, or army on horseback; Kushites retreated south.

#### Meroë Period

- **Meroë:** became capital in 590 B.C.; good location for producing iron
- **Economy:** based on ironwork and trade; traded with Central and East Africa, Arabia, Egypt; traded ivory and gold for iron
- **Culture:** developed written language similar to hieroglyphics; royal tombs built of stone and pyramid-shaped; Kushite kings often mummified
- **Decline and End:** destruction of forests led to decline of iron industry (which requires wood in smelting) and eventual decline of the city; finally destroyed when a king from Aksum to the north conquered Kush.

Name _____     Date _____

**DIRECTIONS: Choose the letter of the *best* answer.**

**Use the map to answer questions 1 and 2.**

**The Kingdom of Kush, 700 B.C.**

1   What *three* bodies of water were important to the kingdom of Kush?

A   Ionian Sea, Black Sea, Nile River

B   Red Sea, Nile River, Aral Sea

C   Mediterranean Sea, Caspian Sea, Nile River

D   Mediterranean Sea, Nile River, Red Sea

2   The Nile River helped the relationship between Kush and Egypt because it

A   made each kingdom dependent on the other.

B   made travel and communication easy.

C   covered the same amount of territory in each.

D   helped people of each kingdom learn to sail.

3   Which *three* Kushite ways of life were similar to Egyptian ways of life?

A   spoken language; houses of mud; ships that sailed on Nile

B   use of iron for weapons; female rulers; dependent on Assyrians

C   hieroglyphics; pyramid-shaped tombs; mummification of kings

D   wall paintings; use of horses in fighting; stone weapons

4   The Kushite king Piankhi changed Egypt's history by

A   conquering Assyria.

B   uniting Kush and Egypt.

C   ruling Egypt from Meroë.

D   using iron weapons to attack Memphis.

5   Why did iron become the basis of the Kushite economy during the Meroë period?

A   Iron was easier to make than bronze.

B   The Assyrians had used iron weapons to take Egypt and parts of Kush.

C   The Kushites did not know how to make bronze weapons.

D   The Kushites used iron slabs as monuments for their kings.

Name _____ Date _____

REVIEW

CALIFORNIA CONTENT
STANDARD 6.2.9

# The Beginning of Written Language

**SPECIFIC OBJECTIVE:** Trace the evolution of language and its written forms.

**Read the summary to answer questions on the next page.**

During the time of hunters and gatherers, spoken language developed because of the need for people to communicate and plan. Written language later arose as a necessary part of city life. For example, merchants needed accounts of debts and payments. The Sumerians and Egyptians both developed writing systems around 3000 B.C.

## Sumerian Writing

- **Development of Sumerian Writing:**
    - —written symbols stood for commonly traded objects
    - —pictographs came to stand for ideas as well as objects (a house might stand for the idea of protection and safety as well as a house)
    - —letters, stylized shapes, came to stand for sounds (whole syllables)
- **Cuneiform:** wedge-shaped letter forms; scribes used pointed stylus to press symbols into moist clay; clay hardened in sun; 600 different symbols; few people could read and write, because of complexity; scribes became official "writers" of Sumerian history; spread throughout Mesopotamia

## Egyptian Writing

- **Beginnings:** Used crude pictographs
- **Improvements:** New form of writing called hieroglyphs (pictures that stand for objects, ideas, and sounds); grew to include over 6,000 symbols
- **Papyrus:** First used stone and clay; later invented papyrus; used tall stalks of papyrus (reed that grew in marshy delta); split reeds into narrow strips; soaked and pressed strips into sheets of paper-like material; dry climate preserved papyrus; modern scholars can still read 5,000-year-old writings
- **Scribes:** people who could write hieroglyphs; required many years of study

## Ancient Texts That Survive:

- **Gilgamesh:** Archaeologists excavated 12 cuneiform tablets that told the story of a cruel and powerful Sumerian king named Gilgamesh.
- **Code of Hammurabi:** More than 3,500 years ago, Hammurabi, a Babylonian king, had 282 laws chiseled into a column of black stone.
- **Assyrian Letters:** Letters were etched on clay tablets in Akkadian, an ancient Mesopotamian language. The letters tell stories of everyday life in Mesopotamia.

**PRACTICE**

CALIFORNIA CONTENT
STANDARD 6.2.9

# The Beginning of Written Language

**DIRECTIONS: Choose the letter of the *best* answer.**

1 Hieroglyphs in ancient Egyptian writing were pictures that stood for
   A whole syllables.
   B debts and payments.
   C kings and gods.
   D objects, sounds, and ideas.

2 The form of Sumerian writing that used a stylus to press shapes in moist clay is called
   A hieroglyphs.
   B pictographs.
   C papyrus.
   D cuneiform.

3 The first writing systems developed in ancient Sumer and ancient Egypt around
   A 5000 B.C.
   B 3000 B.C.
   C 1500 B.C.
   D 500 B.C.

4 Along with hieroglyphics, the Egyptians invented
   A papyrus scrolls.
   B cuneiform.
   C the stylus.
   D an alphabet.

"The sea quieted down; hurricane and storm ceased. I looked out upon the sea and raised loud my voice, But all mankind had turned back into clay."

—from *Assyrian and Babylonian Literature*, edited by Rossiter Johnson

5 The quotation from the ancient Sumerian story, *The Epic of Gilgamesh*, shows that
   A Sumerians knew many languages.
   B complex stories could be told in cuneiform.
   C storytelling began with written language.
   D written language made stories less poetic.

6 In *both* ancient Egypt and ancient Sumer, scribes were few because
   A they were an upper class to which only royalty could belong.
   B most people did not need to communicate complex ideas.
   C papyrus was difficult to obtain.
   D each writing system had many symbols.

**REVIEW**

CALIFORNIA CONTENT
STANDARD 6.3.1

# Origins and Impacts
# of Judaism

**SPECIFIC OBJECTIVE:** Describe the origins and significance of Judaism as the first monotheistic religion based on the concept of one God who sets down moral laws for humanity.

**Read the summary to answer questions on the next page.**

## The Hebrew Bible

The first five books of the Hebrew Bible (Genesis, Exodus, Leviticus, Numbers, and Deuteronomy) are known as the Torah. According to Jewish tradition, God gave the Torah to the Hebrews. The Torah contains an account of the early history of the Hebrew people as well as a description of their laws and beliefs.

## The Beginnings of Judaism

According to the Hebrew Bible, Abraham is the father of the Hebrews. Around 1800 B.C., Abraham lived with his wife, Sarah, and his family of wandering herders in the Sumerian city-state of Ur. Abraham made a covenant (agreement) with God. Abraham promised to follow the laws of the faith and to be righteous and just. In return, God promised to protect the Hebrews and to give them a land of their own.

## Belief in One God

A belief in many Gods is called **polytheism.** A belief in one God is called **monotheism.** (*Poly* and *mono* come from the Greek terms for "many" and "one.") The Hebrews were the first monotheistic people of the ancient world. Their belief in one all-powerful God began with Abraham and his covenant with God. Abraham chose the idea of one God, and God chose Abraham. For this reason, the ancient Hebrews thought of themselves as God's chosen people.

## Significance of Judaism

Monotheism was an important step in the development of world religion. Not only did modern Judaism develop out of the beliefs and practices of the ancient Hebrews, but this first monotheistic religion helped create others as well. Today there are three main monotheistic religions—Christianity, Islam, and Judaism. All three acknowledge Abraham as an important ancestor. Jewish laws and traditions have had an important impact on Western civilization.

**PRACTICE**

CALIFORNIA CONTENT
STANDARD 6.3.1

# Origins and Impacts of Judaism

**DIRECTIONS: Choose the letter of the *best* answer.**

**1  What is the Torah?**

   **A**  the covenant between Abraham and God

   **B**  the original home of the ancient Hebrews

   **C**  the first five books of the Hebrew Bible

   **D**  the history of the Jews

**2  In the writings of the ancient Hebrews, who was Abraham?**

   **A**  the first man created by God

   **B**  the father of the Hebrews, who made a covenant with God

   **C**  a man living in Sumer who worshiped many Gods

   **D**  the great Jewish leader who led the Israelites out of Egypt

**3  What does Abraham promise to do in his covenant with God?**

   **A**  destroy all the people who worship idols

   **B**  follow the laws of God and be righteous and just

   **C**  sacrifice his first-born son to God

   **D**  go to war with those who worshiped idols

**4  What is the difference between polytheism and monotheism?**

   **A**  Polytheists worship one God, while monotheists worship many.

   **B**  Monotheism includes idol worship, while polytheism does not.

   **C**  There is no difference.

   **D**  Monotheists worship one God, while polytheists worship many.

**5  What religion developed directly from the religion of the ancient Hebrews?**

   **A**  Orthodox Christianity

   **B**  Islam

   **C**  modern Christianity

   **D**  modern Judaism

**6  Which are *three* monotheistic religions?**

   **A**  Christianity, Judaism, and Islam

   **B**  Islam, Buddhism, and Christianity

   **C**  Judaism, Islam, and Confucianism

   **D**  Paganism, Buddhism, and Islam

CALIFORNIA CONTENT
STANDARD 6.3.2

# Teachings and Central Beliefs of Judaism

**SPECIFIC OBJECTIVE:** Identify the sources of the ethical teachings and central beliefs of Judaism: belief in God, observance of law, practice of the concepts of righteousness and justice, and the importance of study; and describe how the ideas of the Hebrew traditions are reflected in the moral and ethical traditions of Western civilization.

**Read the summary to answer questions on the next page.**

**Belief in One God**  Judaism is based on the belief that there is one true God. This God is all-powerful, all-knowing, and ever-present.

- The **Covenant** (sacred or holy agreement) between Abraham and God, renewed when God gave the Ten Commandments to Moses, became the basis for the religious laws of Judaism.
- The ancient Hebrews based their laws or covenants on the idea that God is just.
- Many religions had multiple gods, but not all gods were thought to be fair or just.
- Belief in a single God has become the center of Western religious belief.

**Observance of Law**  According to the Torah, Jewish people agreed to live according to God's laws. God gave the laws to the Hebrew people in the Ten Commandments and in the Torah.

- In Judaism, no one is above the law—even Jewish kings had to obey the Torah.
- The idea of a government made of laws, not of rulers, had an impact on Roman law, English law, and eventually the Declaration of Independence, and the U.S. Constitution and Bill of Rights.
- Judaism also set forth concepts known in many democracies today, such as equality before the law and the right to a fair trial.

**Practice of the Righteousness**  The Torah commands that Jews work actively toward the goals of righteousness and justice. Living in a righteous way means not only giving to charity, but working to eliminate poverty and trouble. The emphasis on charity and care that are a part of Judaism are also a part of Christianity and Islam.

**Importance of Study**  Studying God's law and commandments is a sacred duty for religious Jews. In fact, according to Jewish law, studying the Torah is the same as practicing righteousness.

**PRACTICE**

CALIFORNIA CONTENT
STANDARD 6.3.2

# Teachings and Central Beliefs of Judaism

**DIRECTIONS: Choose the letter of the *best* answer.**

> "You shall have no other god to set
> against me."
>
> —Exodus 20:3, (the first commandment),
> New English Bible.

**1** What does the first commandment show about how Judaism differed from other religions at the time and place of the ancient Hebrews?

  **A** In Judaism God could speak, compared with other gods who could not.

  **B** Judaism had only one God, while other religions had many.

  **C** Other religions did not have laws, rules, or commandments.

  **D** Monotheism was more common before Judaism.

**2** Which *two* democratic legal rights have grown out of Jewish tradition?

  **A** the right to remain silent and the right to a lawyer

  **B** equality before the law and the right to a fair trial

  **C** trial by jury and a reasonable bail

  **D** the right to a lawyer and the right to a fair trial

**3** The Torah says Jews must practice righteousness, which includes

  **A** making sure you are right most of the time.

  **B** being careful not to disagree with neighbors.

  **C** telling other people what to do.

  **D** helping others who are in need.

**4** Why is studying God's laws so important to the Jewish people?

  **A** Studying God's laws is the same as being righteous.

  **B** Learning God's laws would help Jews in other lands.

  **C** Knowing the laws makes it possible to convert others to Judaism.

  **D** Ignorance of Jewish law was the reason why Abraham left Sumer.

**5** Which *two* ideas from the Hebrew traditions have become part of the moral and ethical traditions of Western civilization?

  **A** required religious education and the right to a lawyer

  **B** government of laws and belief in one God

  **C** religious intolerance and an obligation to give to charity

  **D** required elementary education for boys and girls and religious tolerance

**REVIEW**

CALIFORNIA CONTENT
STANDARD 6.3.3

*Characters from the Torah and Jewish History*

**SPECIFIC OBJECTIVE:** Explain the significance of Abraham, Moses, Naomi, Ruth, David, and Yohanan ben Zaccai in the development of the Jewish religion.

**Read the summary to answer questions on the next page.**

**Abraham** was a shepherd from the Sumerian city-state of Ur. Jewish tradition holds that, around 1800 B.C., Abraham made a covenant (a promise) to worship and follow only God and Jewish laws. God told Abraham to leave Ur and go to Canaan, along the Mediterranean Sea. Abraham believed that by agreeing to settle in Canaan, the land was promised to his descendents. Abraham is recognized as an important figure in three major religions—Judaism, Christianity, and Islam.

**Moses,** a Hebrew raised as an Egyptian prince, led the Israelites out of slavery. Around 1700 B.C., famine brought hard times to Canaan. Many groups, including Abraham's kin and followers, went to live in Egypt where they became slaves. In the Torah, God chooses Moses to lead his people across the desert to Canaan, the promised land. This journey is known as the Exodus. Moses and his people wandered in the Sinai Desert for 40 years. On Mt. Sinai, Moses received the Ten Commandments from God.

**Naomi and Ruth** were a famously close mother-daughter-in-law pair. According to the Torah, Naomi and her husband went to live in Moab during a famine. After her husband and sons died, Naomi decided to return to the promised land. She told her daughters-in-law to go back to their people in Moab. Out of loyalty, Ruth chose to stay with Naomi. Ruth remarried in Canaan, and one of her descendents, David, became a great king there.

**David** was the second king of the 12 tribes of Israel. He ruled during the 900s B.C. He made Jerusalem the capital of the kingdom and organized a central government.

**Yohanan ben Zaccai** helped preserve Jewish traditions. Beginning in 63 B.C., the Romans ruled the Jews. During this time, a group of Jewish rebels fought to free themselves. The Romans responded by sending in an army led by General Vespasian. Jews feared the Roman troops would destroy their temple. Yohanan ben Zaccai went to ask Vespasian to set aside a place for Jewish scholars to study. Zaccai then set up a school that kept alive Jewish practice. His actions helped preserve Judaism into the future.

**PRACTICE**

CALIFORNIA CONTENT
STANDARD 6.3.3

# Characters from the Torah and Jewish History

---

**DIRECTIONS: Choose the letter of the *best* answer.**

**1** **What role does Abraham play in Judaism, Christianity, and Islam?**

**A** considered the father of the Muslims; no connection to Judaism or Christianity

**B** mentioned in the Hebrew Bible; not known in the Christian or Islamic faiths

**C** founded Judaism and Christianity; not a part of Islam

**D** mentioned in sacred texts of Christianity, Islam, and Judaism

**2** **After the Israelites were enslaved in Egypt, they were led to freedom by**

**A** Ruth.

**B** David.

**C** Abraham.

**D** Moses.

**3** **What did Moses receive from God on Mount Sinai?**

**A** food and water for the Israelites in the desert

**B** ownership of the promised land

**C** the Ten Commandments as God's law

**D** weapons to fight the powerful pharaoh

**4** **What virtue is shown by the story of Naomi and Ruth?**

**A** cleanliness

**B** loyalty

**C** charity

**D** fairness

**5** **King David established the capital of Israel in which city?**

**A** Babylon

**B** Hebron

**C** Ur

**D** Jerusalem

**6** **Why is Yohanan ben Zaccai an important figure in Jewish history?**

**A** He wrote the first written version of the Torah.

**B** His actions helped preserve Jewish learning and traditions.

**C** He fought the Romans who tried to take over Jerusalem.

**D** He protected the temple from destruction.

**REVIEW**

**CALIFORNIA CONTENT STANDARD 6.3.4**

## *Migrations of the Jewish People*

**SPECIFIC OBJECTIVE:** Discuss the locations of the settlements and movements of Hebrew peoples, including the Exodus and their movements to and from Egypt, and outline the significance of the Exodus to the Jewish and other people.

**Read the summary to answer questions on the next page.**

### Drought and famine

Jewish belief says that around 1700 B.C., drought and famine in Canaan forced Abraham's descendents to leave and settle in Egypt. Even in dry years, Egypt had water from its great river, the Nile. At first, the Hebrews had high positions in the Egyptian Kingdom. Later, as the number of Hebrews grew, their presence threatened the Egyptians. As a result, the Egyptians enslaved the Hebrew people.

### The Exodus

According to the Torah, sometime around 1250 B.C., God chose Moses to lead the Hebrews out of captivity in Egypt. The pharaoh did not want to let the Hebrews go free, but God sent ten terrible plagues that eventually changed pharaoh's mind. Moses led his people out of Egypt into the Sinai desert where God gave Moses laws, in the form of the Ten Commandments. The story of Exodus is about leaving slavery and finding freedom and about traveling from a land of oppression to a promised land. Oppressed peoples in many places and times refer to this story of liberation. For example, African Americans newly freed from slavery after the Civil War were able to settle free land in the West. They were part of a movement called the Exodusters.

### From Kingdom to Captivity

Around 1020 B.C., Saul united the Hebrews and became the first in a line of Hebrew kings. The second king, King David, made Jerusalem the capital of Israel. Solomon, the third king, built the first great temple there. When Solomon's son became king, the northern tribes refused to pledge their loyalty. Eventually Israel was divided into two kingdoms—Israel in the north and Judah, which included Jerusalem, in the South. Around 586 B.C., the Babylonians captured Jerusalem and destroyed Solomon's temple. The Jews were forced into exile, or homelessness. Their exile ended in 538 B.C. after Persia captured Babylonia and allowed the Jews to return to Judah, their homeland. Jewish workers completed a new, second, temple in 515 B.C.

**PRACTICE**

**CALIFORNIA CONTENT STANDARD 6.3.4**

*Migrations of the Jewish People*

**DIRECTIONS: Choose the letter of the *best* answer.**

**1** **Why did Abraham's descendents leave Canaan?**

   **A** They were forced by drought to move on.

   **B** God told them to settle in Egypt.

   **C** They wanted to seek their fortunes in better places.

   **D** Canaan had become too crowded.

**2** **What happened to the ancient Hebrews in Egypt?**

   **A** Hebrews were made the high priests of the land.

   **B** The Pharaoh chose Hebrews to be royal servants.

   **C** In time, Hebrews were enslaved by Egyptians.

   **D** Hebrews mingled and intermarried with the Egyptians.

**3** **In 1849, Harriet Tubman escaped slavery and used the Underground Railroad to conduct others to freedom. Why would Tubman have been known as "the Moses of her people"?**

   **A** The South was often called "Egypt" during the 1800s.

   **B** Tubman was given a set of laws by God.

   **C** Both figures led people to freedom from slavery.

   **D** Tubman brought plagues upon her former owners.

"When Israel was in Egypt's land,
'Let my people go!'
Oppressed so hard they could not stand,
'Let my people go!'
Go down, Moses, way down in Egypt's
land, Tell ol' Pharaoh to let my people go!"

—"Go Down, Moses,"
Traditional Spiritual Hymn

**4** **According to the popular hymn, "Go Down, Moses," what connection did African Americans make with the ancient Hebrews?**

   **A** Singing was used to make people feel better in both communities.

   **B** Strong leaders in both communities negotiated an end to bondage.

   **C** Both communities were enslaved in a land that was not their own.

   **D** Both communities journeyed to a new land to make a better life.

**5** **After the Jews returned from exile in Babylonia in 538 B.C. they**

   **A** destroyed the temple built by Solomon.

   **B** went back to worship in the temple built by Solomon.

   **C** restored the temple built by Solomon.

   **D** built a new temple on the site of Solomon's temple.

**REVIEW**

CALIFORNIA CONTENT
STANDARD 6.3.5

## The Jewish Diaspora

**SPECIFIC OBJECTIVE:** Discuss how Judaism survived and developed despite the continuing dispersion of much of the Jewish population from Jerusalem and the rest of Israel after the destruction of the second temple in A.D. 70.

**Read the summary to answer questions on the next page.**

### The Jewish Diaspora

The scattering or dispersal movement of Jews is called the *Diaspora*, a Greek word meaning "scattered."

- **Leaving Judea:** The Diaspora intensified in A.D. 70, when the Romans destroyed the second temple and began to force Jews out of Judea, or Palestine as it came to be called. By about A.D. 500, there were Jewish communities in more than a dozen cities throughout the Mediterranean and beyond.

- **Eastern Europe:** As a religious minority, Jews were often forced to leave a community. By 1900, most Jews were living in Eastern Europe and Russia where they faced poverty and government-led attacks. The majority continued to follow the laws and customs of Judaism.

- **Worldwide:** In 1948, following World War II and the Holocaust, which had targeted Jews for mass killing, the United Nations helped create the state of Israel for Jews to have a traditional homeland. Jews now live around the world, with the largest populations in (from greatest to least) the United States, Israel, France, Russia, Ukraine, Canada, and the United Kingdom.

### Among but Apart

- **Without a Homeland:** In order to maintain their identity, Jews tended to settle together. Sometimes Jews were forced to live in walled Jewish ghettos. The level of tolerance and freedom for Jews has been different in different regions and times.

- **Ongoing Faith:** In every community, Jews have maintained religious traditions, including learning the language and messages of the Torah. Wherever Jews settled, they built synagogues, or temples, in which to worship.

- **The Results of Exile:** Jews adapted to the new places in which they lived. For example, German Jews developed a language called Yiddish—a mixture of Hebrew and German. Some Jews in the Diaspora have given up traditional and religious customs, but maintain connections to their past. Others have established lives that promote the special foods, daily prayers, and other religious practices commanded in the Torah.

**PRACTICE**

CALIFORNIA CONTENT
STANDARD 6.3.5

# The Jewish Diaspora

**DIRECTIONS: Choose the letter of the *best* answer.**

**1** ***One*** **way Jews of the Diaspora kept their identity was by**

A keeping their children out of schools.

B obeying only Jewish law, not local law.

C continuing to study the Torah.

D helping non-Jews to learn Yiddish.

**2** **For the Jewish communities of the Diaspora, synagogues were**

A places of worship and learning.

B centers of government.

C schools to learn new local customs.

D courthouses for Jewish law.

**3** **After the Diaspora, Jews continued moving toward Eastern Europe and Russia because they**

A wanted to see other parts of Europe and Russia.

B followed rumors of a gold rush in Siberia.

C wanted to convert Russians and Europeans to Judaism.

D were forced to move by discrimination and cruelty.

**4** **What event in 70 A.D. increased the movement of Jews to other parts of the world?**

A the destruction of the second temple by the Romans

B the exile of the Jews into Babylon

C the birth of Jesus Christ

D the defeat of the Babylonians by the Persians

**5** **What are the *three* countries with the largest Jewish populations today?**

A Israel, United States, and Canada

B Ukraine, Israel, and Canada

C Israel, France, and Ukraine

D United States, Israel, and France

**6** **What does the establishment of Israel in 1948 mean to the Jews?**

A Jews can speak Yiddish whenever and wherever they want.

B Jews have a homeland where they can practice Judaism without fear.

C Muslims and Christians are not allowed into the Jewish homeland.

D All Jews from around the world must immigrate to the homeland.

Name _____     Date _____

**REVIEW**

**CALIFORNIA CONTENT
STANDARD 6.4.1**

# *The Greek City-States*

**SPECIFIC OBJECTIVE:** Discuss the connections between geography and the development of city-states in the region of the Aegean Sea, including patterns of trade and commerce among Greek city-states and within the wider Mediterranean region.

**Read the summary to answer questions on the next page.**

In ancient times, Greece was not a united country. The mountains and sea divided Greece into many parts. Yet everywhere in the country, people lived in similar ways.

## The Sea and Islands

- Mainland Greece is a large peninsula jutting into the Mediterranean Sea.
- Peloponnesus is a small peninsula at the southern tip of Greece, nearly cut off from the rest of the country by the narrow Gulf of Corinth.
- The Mediterranean, Ionian, and Aegean Seas were links that united Greek people.
- Thousands of Greek islands spread like stepping stones across the Aegean Sea.

## Landforms and Inland Waters

- Mountains cover about three-fourths of Greece, dividing it into different regions, making transportation and farming difficult.
- Tiny, fertile valleys cover about one-fourth of Greece.
- Rivers in Greece are narrow and shallow, slowing transportation.

## Government and Trade

- By 700 B.C., city-states arose in Greece. The Greek word for a city-state is *polis*. A polis included a city and the land around it.
- Because of rugged mountain terrain, city-states were isolated from each other and developed independent governments rather than one unified government.
- For many years, Greek farmers grew enough to feed the people, but as population numbers grew, food became more scarce.
- The ancient Greeks traded products, such as oil, that were in demand elsewhere. Oil was used to light lamps and to cook. Greeks exchanged oil for grains and also sold wine, wool, and pottery.
- Grains, timber, nuts, figs, and cheese were purchased from outside Greek city-states.
- The ancient Greeks learned a written alphabet from Phoenicians and the use of coin money through trade.

**PRACTICE**

CALIFORNIA CONTENT
STANDARD 6.4.1

# The Greek City-States

**DIRECTIONS: Choose the letter of the *best* answer.**

1 City-states developed in ancient Greece because the
   A cities became states as they grew larger.
   B rivers were so wide, states formed on opposite banks.
   C mountains isolated the country into separate regions.
   D people did not believe in obeying kings.

2 *Polis* is the Greek word for
   A peninsula.
   B city-state.
   C population.
   D war ship.

3 Three-fourths of Greece is covered by
   A cities.
   B oceans.
   C deserts.
   D mountains.

4 *One* reason that the ancient Greeks traded with other countries was their need for
   A olive oil.
   B grain.
   C wine.
   D pottery.

5 The peninsula at the southern tip of Greece, which is connected to the mainland by a narrow isthmus, is called
   A the Agean.
   B Athens.
   C Peloponnesus.
   D Sicily.

**REVIEW**

**CALIFORNIA CONTENT STANDARD 6.4.2**

# Government in Ancient Greece

**SPECIFIC OBJECTIVE:** Trace the transition from tyranny and oligarchy to early democratic forms of government and back to dictatorship in ancient Greece, including the significance of the invention of the idea of citizenship.

**Read the summary to answer questions on the next page.**

## Forms of Government in Ancient Greece

Because the city-states in ancient Greece were independent, each one developed its own political system. Most governments in Greece gradually changed from one ruler to rule by citizens. In Greece, the freedom to express ideas and the willingness of leaders to listen was accepted as a way of life.

**Monarchy**: In a monarchy, a single royal figure holds supreme power. Most city-states began as monarchies, but changed over time.

**Aristocracy:** An aristocracy is ruled by nobles, or the upper class. In Greece, aristocracies gained control during the 700s B.C. These governments were more inclusive and often more fair than rule by monarchs.

**Oligarchy:** Oligarchies, rule by wealthy landowners, replaced aristocracies. For the first time, people had a voice in government.

**Tyrants:** By 650 B.C., tyrants had replaced oligarchies. Today the word *tyrant* describes a cruel leader; in ancient Greece, a tyrant was a powerful, but fair, ruler. Some tyrants even helped the poor by providing jobs or forgiving debts.

## Pericles and Early Democracy

- The first city-state to build democracy was Athens, in southeast Greece.
- The most important governing group in Athens was the assembly.
- In the Greek assembly, every citizen had the right to vote, but not all people were citizens. Athenian citizenship was limited to free men, native to Athens, who were at least 18 years old.
- Pericles ruled Athens during a Golden Age (461–429 B.C.), in which democracy and the arts flourished. He offered payment for government jobs so poor citizens could hold office.

## End of Democracy

- Two city-states, Athens and Sparta, fought for control of Greece during the Peloponnesian War.
- Weakened by war, King Philip of Macedonia, ruler of a kingdom to the north, conquered Greece in 336 B.C. Under Philip's rule, democracy in Greece ended.

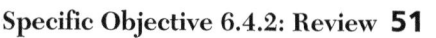

**PRACTICE**

CALIFORNIA CONTENT
STANDARD 6.4.2

# Government in Ancient Greece

**DIRECTIONS: Choose the letter of the *best* answer.**

**1** A government ruled by a group of landowners is called

**A** a tyrant.

**B** an oligarchy.

**C** a dictatorship.

**D** a monarchy.

"When a citizen is in any way distinguished, he is preferred to the public servant [politician], not as a matter of privilege, but as the reward of merit."

—"Funeral Oration," Pericles, from
*The History of the Peloponnesian War*
by Thucydides

**2** Though the quotation is from a speech given at a soldier's funeral, Pericles's topic is not war, but the

**A** threat of conquest.

**B** history of oligarchies.

**C** virtues of democracy.

**D** cruelty of tyrants.

**3** Democracy in ancient Greece was ended by

**A** Alexander the Great.

**B** Sparta.

**C** Solon.

**D** Philip of Macedonia.

**4** During the 700s B.C., what form of government replaced monarchies in ancient Greece?

**A** tyrants

**B** aristocracies

**C** monarchs

**D** democracies

**5** The Athenian ruler Pericles promoted the rights of poor people by giving them

**A** paid government jobs.

**B** citizenship, even if they were foreign-born.

**C** their own enslaved workers.

**D** the right to be wealthy nobles.

**6** In ancient Greece, the change from one government to another usually indicated a desire for

**A** tyrants to rule.

**B** nobles to increase their rights.

**C** more people to have a say in government.

**D** Greeks to be ruled by one person rather than many.

**REVIEW**

CALIFORNIA CONTENT
STANDARD 6.4.3

# *Direct and Representative Democracy*

***

**SPECIFIC OBJECTIVE:** State the key differences between Athenian, or direct, democracy and representative democracy.

**Read the summary to answer questions on the next page.**

## Athenian (Direct) Democracy

- **Direct democracy,** or participatory democracy, was practiced in Athens and other Greek city-states from 500 to 300 B.C.

- All citizens participated directly in government. However, not all Athenians were citizens—citizenship belonged to males 18 years and over, who had been born in Athens and whose parents had also been born there. (Immigrants, women, and enslaved people were excluded.)

- Made up of three branches of government: Executive (the elected leader) carried out laws; Assembly (made up of all citizens) proposed and passed laws; Judicial held trials.

- Athenian democracy depended on citizens being willing to participate in government, to fight to defend Athens, and to place community needs above their own.

## Representative Democracy

- Representative democracy is practiced in many countries today, including the United States. In some countries (such as the U.S.), representative democracy is called a **republic.**

- Political power is held by all citizens; however, citizens do not make the laws. Instead, they choose representatives. If enough people do not like the laws, they can vote representatives out of office.

- Representative democracies have three branches: Executive: enforces the laws; Legislative: makes the laws; Judicial: explains the laws and makes sure they are fair.

- Representative democracy depends on fair elections, freedom of speech, and a free press.

## Representative Democracy in the United States

- Executive Branch: President elected directly by people

- Legislative Branch: Senate and House of Representatives elected directly by people to represent citizens in making laws

- Judicial Branch: Supreme Court chosen by the president with the advice and consent of Senate

**PRACTICE**

CALIFORNIA CONTENT
STANDARD 6.4.3

# Direct and Representative Democracy

**DIRECTIONS: Choose the letter of the *best* answer.**

**1** The form of democracy that began in Athens around 500 B.C. and influences government today is

  **A** representative.

  **B** legislative.

  **C** direct.

  **D** judicial.

**2** Democracy in the United States has three branches of government. Direct democracy had

  **A** only one branch.

  **B** two branches.

  **C** three branches as well.

  **D** as many branches as there were citizens.

**3** In direct democracy in ancient Greece, which branch of government proposed and passed laws directly?

  **A** the citizen

  **B** the judicial branch

  **C** the executive branch

  **D** the assembly

**4** A citizen who is *not* an elected representative who plans to propose and vote on a new law would have to be a citizen of

  **A** a republic.

  **B** a direct democracy.

  **C** any type of democracy.

  **D** a representative democracy.

**5** If you were 18 and a male in ancient Athens, and you had been born there, you still were not a citizen unless you

  **A** had parents who were citizens.

  **B** knew how to read and write.

  **C** were married.

  **D** owned land.

**6** What quality in citizens is *most* directly linked to a direct democracy?

  **A** the ability to read and write

  **B** technological knowledge

  **C** being community-minded

  **D** ownership of land

Name _____  Date _____

**REVIEW**

CALIFORNIA CONTENT
STANDARD 6.4.4

*Greek Literature*

**SPECIFIC OBJECTIVE:** Explain the significance of Greek mythology to the everyday life of people in the region and how Greek literature continues to permeate our literature and language today, drawing from Greek mythology and epics, such as Homer's *Iliad* and *Odyssey,* and from *Aesop's Fables.*

**Read the summary to answer questions on the next page.**

## Mythology

- The Greeks believed in many gods and imagined the gods to be human-like. Greek gods struggled with weaknesses, like humans, but were immortal—able to live forever.

- Greek myths told stories about gods and heroes. Through these myths, Greeks tried to understand the world around them. Greek myths gave us many English words, such as *atlas, herculean, echo,* and *marathon.*

- Twelve gods and goddesses lived on Mt. Olympus, the highest mountain in Greece. Each city-state had its own special god. For example, Athena, goddess of wisdom, was protector of Athens.

- Greeks erected statues, built temples, and held festivals to honor the gods.

- In war, Greek heroes sought glory. In peace, they held athletic games, including the first Olympics. The Olympics were held every four years in honor of Zeus, the king of gods.

**Homer:** The Greeks were great storytellers. A single tale might be told over several evenings. Such long heroic tales are called **epics.** The greatest of the Greek storytellers was a blind poet named Homer. Homer's two greatest epics are the *Iliad* and the *Odyssey.*

• **The *Iliad*** is an epic poem that tells of several weeks of action during the Trojan War, fought over a woman named Helen, whom the Trojans had kidnapped. The action takes place outside the walls of the ancient city of Troy. The poem describes clashes between great heroes and explores how the tragedy of war affects families and friends. Other poets also composed stories about the Trojan War. From these stories, we get expressions that are still used today, such as "Achilles' heel," "the face that launched a thousand ships," and "Trojan horse."

• **The *Odyssey*** follows the Greek hero Odysseus, who spent ten years after the war finding his way back home. Today, the word *odyssey* means "a long and difficult journey." Some characters in the story are famous, such as the one-eyed cyclops and the singing sirens.

**Aesop's Fables:** Aesop is a legendary storyteller from ancient Greece. Fables teach lessons through short stories about animals, always ending with a moral. The moral of Aesop's "The Fox and the Grapes" is, "It is easy to hate what you cannot have." Another well known fable is "The Tortoise and the Hare," from which comes the familiar saying, "Slow and steady wins the race."

Copyright © McDougal Littell/Houghton Mifflin Company

**PRACTICE**

**CALIFORNIA CONTENT STANDARD 6.4.4**

*Greek Literature*

**DIRECTIONS: Choose the letter of the *best* answer.**

1  "The Fox and the Grapes" is an example of a

   A  myth.

   B  epic.

   C  fable.

   D  poem.

2  The Olympics, which honored Zeus and occured every four years, were named after

   A  a Greek athlete and war-hero.

   B  a minor god.

   C  Zeus's mountain home.

   D  a Greek king.

3  Homer, though he was blind, is famous for creating

   A  two well-known epic poems.

   B  a collection of statues.

   C  fables with morals.

   D  a complete history of Greek kings.

4  The word *odyssey* comes from

   A  the name of the Trojan who kidnapped Helen.

   B  the hero who spent ten years trying to get home to Greece.

   C  a mountain in Greece where the gods lived.

   D  Aesop's fable about the race between the tortoise and the hare.

5  The Greeks believed in many gods and thought them to be

   A  animals, like the Egyptian gods.

   B  very removed from Greek life.

   C  like humans.

   D  easy to ignore.

**REVIEW**

CALIFORNIA CONTENT
STANDARD 6.4.5

*The Persian Empire*

---

**SPECIFIC OBJECTIVE:** Outline the founding, expansion, and political organization of the Persian Empire.

**Read the summary to answer questions on the next page.**

Although the Greeks shared a common culture, each city-state was like its own country. City-states rarely worked together, yet many Greeks wondered how long the city-states could remain independent. The country that most threatened Greece was Persia, located east of Greece in Central Asia. (Today Persia is known as Iran.) By 490 B.C., Persia had taken over most of Southwest Asia and part of North Africa. Then Darius I, the king of Persia, turned his attention to Greece.

## Founding of the Persian Empire

- In 1000 B.C., Persians entered Central Asia. They built tiny kingdoms and traded horses and minerals across Asia.

- **Cyrus the Great,** a brilliant, powerful, and ambitious Persian king, wanted to create a larger empire. He began by conquering what is now Turkey, took former Assyrian and Chaldean lands between 550 and 539 B.C., and ruled with a policy of **toleration,** allowing people to practice their own customs. This made governing the large empire much easier.

## Expanding the Empire

- Darius I took control in 490 B.C., squashing rebellions and conquering new lands.
- Darius controlled a vast empire—around 2,800 miles from east to west.
- The Persian Empire at this time was so large that Darius divided it into 20 provinces.

## Political Organization

- **Government:** Each province had a governor, called a **satrap,** who carried out the emperor's orders and collected taxes. Each satrap had a military commander to help. Spies were sent out to ensure the satraps were obedient to the emperor.

- **Royal Road:** A road 1,775 miles long was built to send royal messages throughout the Empire. Messengers could get fresh horses at relay stations, every 15 miles along the road. It took seven days to travel from one end of the empire to the other. Military troops and mail messengers also traveled along the road.

- **Laws and Currency:** Persians minted coins, which they learned from the Lydians, a conquered people. Coins promoted business and made tax-paying easier. The empire also used a law code based on Hammurabi's Code from Babylonia.

Name _____ Date _____

**PRACTICE**

CALIFORNIA CONTENT
STANDARD 6.4.5

# The Persian Empire

**DIRECTIONS: Choose the letter of the *best* answer.**

**1** Which country to the east threatened the Greek city-states around 500 B.C.?

  **A** Egypt

  **B** China

  **C** Persia

  **D** Turkey

**2** *One* thing that made Cyrus the Great successful was his policy of

  **A** minting coins.

  **B** toleration.

  **C** provincial government.

  **D** torture.

**3** In ancient Persia, a *satrap* was a

  **A** governor.

  **B** cart.

  **C** coin.

  **D** province.

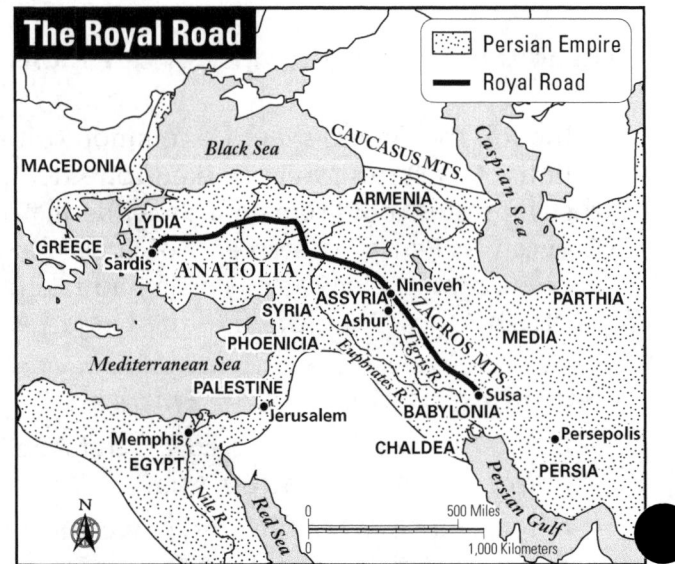

**4** According to the map, the Royal Road connected Susa in the east to which city in the west?

  **A** Babylon

  **B** Ninevah

  **C** Sardis

  **D** Ninevah

**5** The person *most* responsible for founding the Persian Empire was

  **A** Darius I.

  **B** Sardis.

  **C** Cyrus the Great.

  **D** Memphis.

Name _____ Date _____

**REVIEW**

CALIFORNIA CONTENT
STANDARD 6.4.6

*Athens and Sparta*

**SPECIFIC OBJECTIVE:** Compare and contrast life in Athens and Sparta, with emphasis on their roles in the Persian and Peloponnesian Wars.

**Read the chart and summaries to answer questions on the next page.**

| | Athens | Sparta |
|---|---|---|
| **Government** | Direct Democracy; two law-making bodies: Council of Four Hundred and Assembly; all citizens vote on laws | Part monarchy; part oligarchy; part democracy; two kings, five supervisors; Council of Elders; all citizens vote on laws. |
| **Values** | Social, arts, democracy | Military—army and soldiers |
| **Classes** | Four classes, based on income | Citizens; free noncitizens of nearby villages; helots (enslaved people). |
| **Citizens** | Males over 18 served in army and on juries; foreigners, women, children and slaves could not be citizens | Lived in city; spent all their time in military training; men served in army from age 20 to age 60. |
| **Education** | Wealthy boys at age 7 began studies of logic, public speaking, reading, writing, poetry, arithmetic, music, athletics | Boys at age 7 began military life: discipline, duty, strength (little reading). Girls were given athletic and self-defense training. |
| **Women** | Wives, mothers, priestesses; limited property ownership; limited freedom | Trained for strength; owned property; more freedom than in Greece. |

## Persian War

- **First War:** In 490 B.C., Persian forces arrived on the plain of Marathon, 26 miles north of Athens. Athens sent a runner to Sparta for help. The Spartans came too late, but Athenians, though outnumbered, triumphed. The Persians lost 6,400 fighters; The Greeks lost 192.

- **Second War:** In 480 B.C., Persia invaded again, killing 300 Spartan guards at Thermopylae but giving Athenians time to act. They fled their city and sailed to the nearby island of Salamis. There, in a narrow strait, small, swift Greek boats defeated the huge Persian fleet.

- **Athenian victory** preserved Greek democracy against rule by Persian monarchs. Athens entered a Golden Age led by Pericles, whom the Athenians reelected year after year.

## Peloponnesian War

- **Causes:** Some Greeks thought Athens was becoming too ambitious. Athens grew from a city-state to an empire. Athenian settlers moved into the lands of other states.

- **Athens vs. Sparta:** Sparta declared war on Athens in 431 B.C., in what was known as the Peloponnesian War. Athens had a stronger navy; Sparta had a stronger land force. Sparta cut off Athens's food supply by destroying crops. Athens focused on sea battles.

- **Outcome:** Pericles gathered people in Athens, but crowded conditions allowed disease to break out, killing about one third of the population. Athens finally surrendered to Sparta in 404 B.C. The 27-year war had weakened all the city-states.

**PRACTICE**

**CALIFORNIA CONTENT STANDARD 6.4.6**

## *Athens and Sparta*

**DIRECTIONS: Choose the letter of the *best* answer.**

**1** *One* of the ways Sparta differed from Athens was in its focus on
  **A** democracy.
  **B** learning.
  **C** the military.
  **D** sailing.

**2** If you were an independent woman in ancient Greece, you were probably better off living in
  **A** Thebes.
  **B** Sparta.
  **C** Athens.
  **D** Corinth.

**3** The Persian Wars were won by
  **A** Athens.
  **B** Thebes.
  **C** Corinth.
  **D** Sparta.

**4** The overall cause of the Peloponnesian War was
  **A** Sparta's greed.
  **B** Persia's desire for revenge.
  **C** a slave uprising.
  **D** that Athens had become too powerful.

**5** Though Athens and Sparta fought against each other for 27 years in the Peloponnesian War, they were allies in the
  **A** golden age.
  **B** Delian League.
  **C** Olympics.
  **D** Persian Wars.

**REVIEW**

CALIFORNIA CONTENT
STANDARD 6.4.7

# Alexander the Great

**SPECIFIC OBJECTIVE:** Trace the rise of Alexander the Great and the spread of Greek culture eastward and into Egypt.

**Read the summary to answer questions on the next page.**

After the Athenians' defeat in the Peloponnesian War, it seemed that the Greeks would never again be united. In time, Greece was invaded by Phillip II of Macedonia.

## Macedonia

- Home of a fierce, warlike people, who lived north of Greece
- Philip II came to throne in 359 B.C.; he had admired Greece since his boyhood there.
- Built large army and defeated one Greek city-state after another
- Before final victory, Philip died, leaving the empire to his 20-year-old son Alexander.

## Alexander the Great

- Continued father's plans to build empire
- Quelled uprising in Greek city-state of Thebes as an example to Greeks
- Took over Egypt peacefully; became pharaoh
- Attacked Persepolis, capital of Persia; by 331 B.C. (age 25), controlled Persian Empire
- Marched to the Indus River Valley, wanting to go further east, but army refused
- Died of fever in Babylon at age 32 on his way home to Macedonia

## Hellenistic Age

- Kingdom created by Alexander lasted 200 years, known as Hellenistic Age.
- *Hellenistic* means "Greek-like."
- People in empire blended Greek culture with their own; Greek became common language throughout empire; Hellenistic art, architecture, philosophy, and science showed influence of many cultures, but roots were clearly Greek.

## Alexandria

- Blending of Greek ideas was centered in Alexandria, located on Egypt's Nile Delta.
- Important center of learning until 200 A.D.
- Scholars from all over the empire studied there.
- Temple of the Muses, a museum of the arts and sciences, named after Greek goddesses who ruled over arts and sciences
- Home to one of the Seven Wonders of the World—a lighthouse seen for 35 miles

Name _____ Date _____

# Alexander the Great

**DIRECTIONS: Choose the letter of the *best* answer.**

1  How did Philip II of Macedonia react toward Greek culture when he came to power in 359 B.C.?

   A  was offended by anything Greek

   B  wanted to destroy Greek culture

   C  admired Greek culture

   D  had no strong feelings toward Greek culture

2  The Hellenistic Age refers to the period in history when

   A  Alexander's kingdom, which lasted 200 years, blended other cultures with Greek culture.

   B  Pericles ruled Athens and made it the center of Greek learning and culture.

   C  Alexander ruled Egypt and built Alexandria, a center of Greek culture.

   D  Philip II of Macedonia defeated one Greek city-state after another.

3  How did Alexander the Great take control of Egypt?

   A  peacefully

   B  by destroying its capital city

   C  by assassinating the king

   D  by winning a lengthy war

4  Which city-state did Alexander destroy in order to intimidate the Greeks?

   A  Athens

   B  Corinth

   C  Sparta

   D  Thebes

5  Alexandria, an important center of learning in Hellenistic culture, was located in

   A  Egypt.

   B  Greece.

   C  India.

   D  Persia.

**REVIEW**

CALIFORNIA CONTENT
STANDARD 6.4.8

*The Greek Legacy*

**SPECIFIC OBJECTIVE:** Describe the enduring contributions of important Greek figures in the arts and sciences.

### Read the summary to answer questions on the next page.

### Drama

- Greeks invented drama as an art form and were the first to build theaters.
- Tragedy was the first form of drama, portraying men and women of character whose very strength led to downfall.
- Comedy was a lesser form, usually making fun of political leaders or ideas.
- Sophocles—Important Greek dramatist; wrote famous play *Oedipus Rex*, a tragedy about a good king who kills the man he later learns was his father
- Aristophanes—Famous comedic playwright whose play, *The Birds*, made fun of people who are hungry for power

### Sculpture and Architecture

- Sculptors—portrayed ideal; most works were outdoors or in temples
- Greek architecture—Ionic, Corinthian, and Doric columns
- Parthenon—Built as temple for goddess Athena; had roof supported by marble columns; inside was statue of Athena, made of gold, ivory, and gems

### History

- Greek historians—One of first cultures to write their own history
- Herodotus—"Father of History"; wrote *History*, an account of Persian Wars
- Thucydides—Wrote *History of Peloponnesian War* using eyewitness accounts

### Philosophy

- Philosophers—Sought knowledge and wisdom; asked abstract questions such as, "What is truth?"; believed universe was orderly and governed by laws
- Socrates—Developed question-and-answer style of teaching, still in use; called the Socratic Method
- Plato—Student of Socrates; wrote *The Republic*, a book about ideal government ruled by wise philosopher-kings; started school called "The Academy," which ran for 900 years
- Aristotle—Student of Plato; invented method of debate based on rules of logic; opened school called "The Lyceum" in Athens; tutored Alexander the Great

### Astronomy, Mathematics, and Physics

- Astronomers—Made important discoveries about planets and stars
- Ptolemy—Put Earth at center of universe, a belief that remained for 1,400 years
- Euclid—Famed mathematician who developed geometry
- Archimedes—Invented law of lever; compound pulley
- Hypatia—First famous female mathematician; also a teacher and astronomer

**PRACTICE**

CALIFORNIA CONTENT
STANDARD 6.4.8

## The Greek Legacy

**DIRECTIONS: Choose the letter of the *best* answer.**

**1** The Greeks' first drama form was the

   **A** skit.

   **B** comedy.

   **C** tragedy.

   **D** epic.

**2** What was the Parthenon in ancient Greece?

   **A** a temple for the goddess Athena

   **B** a famous Greek tragedy

   **C** a book written by the philosopher Plato

   **D** a type of Greek column

**3** Which Greek philosopher founded a famous academy that was in operation for 900 years?

   **A** Aristotle

   **B** Plato

   **C** Socrates

   **D** Herodotus

**4** Hypatia and Euclid are examples of ancient Greek

   **A** dramatists.

   **B** historians.

   **C** mathematicians.

   **D** philosophers.

**5** Alexander the Great's most famous tutor was

   **A** Aristotle.

   **B** Herodotus.

   **C** Plato.

   **D** Socrates.

"The Athenians . . . fell upon them, and fought in a manner worthy of being recorded. They were the first of the Greeks, so far as I know, who introduced the custom of charging the enemy at a run. . . ."

— from *The History of Herodotus*, translated by George Rawlinson

**6** The quotation from Herodotus shows why he became known as

   **A** a writer of comedy skits.

   **B** a great inventor.

   **C** Plato's greatest pupil.

   **D** the father of history.

Name _____     Date _____

**CALIFORNIA CONTENT
STANDARD 6.5.1**

*Early Indian River Cultures*

**SPECIFIC OBJECTIVE:** Locate and describe the major river system and discuss the physical setting that supported the rise of this civilization.

**Read the summary to answer questions on the next page.**

### Geography

- **Mountains:** The Hindu Kush to the west and the Himalayas to the east form much of India's northern border.
- **Rivers:** India has several great rivers, including the Ganges and Indus. Rivers carry water for irrigation. The silt deposited by the rivers makes the land along them fertile. The Saraswati River ran parallel to the Indus River but dried up, perhaps due to an earthquake.
- **Climate:** Mountain ranges block cold northern winds, creating a warm climate. Seasonal monsoon winds bring dry weather in the winter and rain in the summer.

### Indus Valley Culture

- **Indus River:** The river flows southwest from the Himalayas through present-day Pakistan. Like the Nile River and the Tigris-Euphrates River, the Indus floods every year, providing a rich layer of soil.
- **Farming Villages:** Early settlements were villages where people earned their living from the land and domesticated cattle, sheep, goats, and chickens.
- **Cities:** Workers wove raw cotton into cloth. Others worked as carpenters, merchants, and teachers. There were also scribes for writing. Artisans created tools from copper and bronze.

### Harappan Civilization

- Located in the Indus and Saraswati river valleys, covering an area twice the size of Texas
- Consisted of hundreds of cities, all with a common design
- The largest cities, Harappa and Mohenjo-Daro, had at least 35,000 inhabitants each.
- Homes were made of hard-baked bricks; each had a bathroom and toilet, with underground sewers connecting them.
- Writing was based on pictographs that no one in modern times has been able to read.

Copyright © McDougal Littell/Houghton Mifflin Company

CSS Specific Objective 6.5.1: Review **65**

**PRACTICE**

CALIFORNIA CONTENT
STANDARD 6.5.1

*Early Indian River Cultures*

**DIRECTIONS: Choose the letter of the *best* answer.**

1 **What effect do the mountain ranges in the north have on the climate of the Indian subcontinent?**

   A They shade it, keeping it cool.

   B They cause floods every spring when snow melts.

   C They shield it from cold northern winds.

   D They are too far away to have any effect.

2 ***One* important river for early Indian civilizations was the Saraswati River, which today**

   A is much smaller.

   B is too dangerous to live near.

   C has merged with the Ganges.

   D no longer exists.

3 **What method of writing did Harappan Civilization use and what do we know about it today?**

   A similar to cuneiform of the Sumerians; some has been translated

   B similar to Egyptian hieroglyphics, which people today are able to translate

   C no real writing system; no one today knows why

   D form of writing based on pictographs, which no one can read today

4 **The Harappan civilization, located in the Indus and Saraswati river valleys, covered an area of about what size?**

   A half the size of Florida

   B twice as big as Texas

   C a little smaller than Colorado

   D the size of Africa

5 ***One* of the things cities in the Harappan civilization had in common with modern cities was**

   A skyscrapers.

   B wooden houses.

   C indoor plumbing.

   D traffic jams.

6 **What was *one* unique feature of the Harappan civilization?**

   A The cities were all built at the same time.

   B All the houses faced the East.

   C All the cities were built according to a common design.

   D The houses were up on stilts to protect them from flooding.

**REVIEW**

**CALIFORNIA CONTENT STANDARD 6.5.2**

*The Aryan Migrations*

**SPECIFIC OBJECTIVE:** Discuss the significance of the Aryan migrations.

### Read the summary to answer questions on the next page.

The towering, snow-capped mountains that separate India from the rest of Asia look as if they would keep the Indians safe from invasion. Yet over the centuries, one group after another has entered India. One of the most important groups were the Aryans, who came from central Asia.

### Who were the Aryans?

- **Origins:** Some historians believe that the Aryans were part of a larger group they refer to as Indo-Europeans. The Aryans traveled across the Khyber Pass in the Hindu-Kush Mountains. They entered India around 1500 B.C., probably after the Harappan civilization had already fallen. Aryans may have been driven from their homeland by drought, plague, or invasion.

- **Ways of Life:** The Aryans were not city-dwellers. Instead, they herded cattle, sheep, and goats and lived in simple houses in family groups or clans. They spoke Sanskrit, an early Indo-European language.

- **Three classes:** Aryans divided themselves into three classes: warriors, priests, and commoners. The fierce warrior class rode in horse-driven chariots and fought with long bows and arrows and bronze axes.

- **Migrations** by Aryans happened gradually over 1250 years.

- **Aryans settled** throughout the Indian subcontinent over time.

### How did Aryans affect the region?

- **A Blending:** Aryan language and religion were adopted by people already living in area (Dravidians). Aryans learned about agriculture and city life from Dravidians. The interaction of the two cultures led to a complex, blended culture.

- **Religion:** The Aryan religion, Brahmanism, was originally divided into three groups. Over hundreds of years, these three groups expanded into more groups. Brahmanism merged with the religion of others and eventually led to Hinduism.

- **Caste System:** In time, the people of India came to believe that every person is born into his or her special group, or position in life. This way of structuring society is called the caste system.

**A Historical Mystery:** Scientists used to think that the Aryans conquered people already living in the region. It is now agreed that the migration was slow and peaceful. Many mysteries about early civilization in this part of the world remain.

**PRACTICE**

**CALIFORNIA CONTENT STANDARD 6.5.2**

*The Aryan Migrations*

---

**DIRECTIONS: Choose the letter of the *best* answer.**

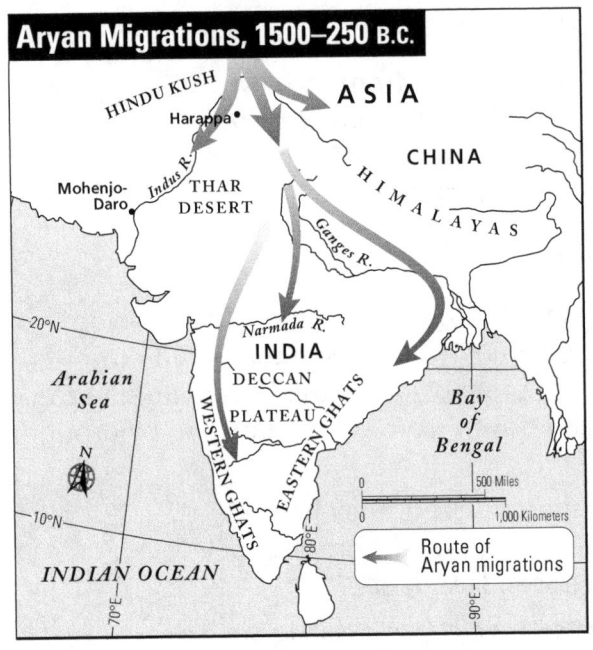

Aryan Migrations, 1500–250 B.C.

HINDU KUSH
Harappa
ASIA
CHINA
Mohenjo-Daro
Indus R.
THAR DESERT
HIMALAYAS
Ganges R.
20°N
Narmada R.
INDIA
DECCAN
Arabian Sea
N
PLATEAU
WESTERN GHATS
EASTERN GHATS
Bay of Bengal
0    500 Miles
0    1,000 Kilometers
10°N
INDIAN OCEAN
70°E
80°E
90°E
← Route of Aryan migrations

**1** **According to the map, how did the Aryans first enter India?**

   **A** south, from China, through the Himalayas

   **B** across the Deccan Plateau in central India

   **C** through the Hindu-Kush Mountains

   **D** from the Himalayas, across the Ganges River

**2** ***One* unique thing the Aryans contributed to the people already living in India was the Aryan**

   **A** language.

   **B** knowledge of agriculture.

   **C** architecture.

   **D** method of planned cities.

**3** **The Aryan class system that eventually developed into India's caste system began with which *three* classes of society?**

   **A** kings, merchants, and commoners

   **B** nobles, landowners, and enslaved people

   **C** commoners, enslaved people, and warriors

   **D** warriors, priests, and commoners

**4** **In the Aryan way of life, Sanskrit was the**

   **A** name for the warrior class.

   **B** early class system.

   **C** language.

   **D** religion.

**5** ***One* reason scientists are not sure whether the Aryans invaded India or settled there peacefully is because**

   **A** Aryan histories tell different stories.

   **B** no one can read the original inhabitants' language.

   **C** there is no evidence of an earlier civilization.

   **D** there is little evidence of an Aryan civilization.

**CALIFORNIA CONTENT STANDARD 6.5.3**

# The Roots of Hinduism

**SPECIFIC OBJECTIVE:** Explain the major beliefs and practices of Brahmanism in India and how they evolved into early Hinduism.

**Read the summary to answer questions on the next page.**

## Brahmanism

- Early Aryan religion; named for Aryan priests, or Brahmins
- Believed in many gods, connected with nature
- Made animal sacrifices over sacred fires
- Ceremonies became longer and more complicated with time.
- Vedas—ancient sacred Sanskrit texts—recorded rituals and hymns.

## Changes to Brahmanism

- **In the Beginning:** Brahmanism made Indians begin to share ideas about the origin of world. This thinking led to changes in Brahmanism.
- **Major Change:** Ancient people developed a belief in one spirit ruling the universe.
- **Ancient Texts:** Indians wrote their ancient history in such works as the *Mahabharata*, an epic poem that retells many legends. The *Bhagavad Gita*, One of Hinduism's most sacred texts, is part of the *Mahabharata*.
- **Hinduism:** A religion that grew out of Brahmanism. The sacred texts of Hinduism include the *Vedas* and the *Puranas*.

## Hinduism

- **Many Deities:** Hindus believe in many deities that are all part of one supreme life force. Hinduism has three most important deities: Brahma, the creator; Vishnu, the protector; and Shiva, the destroyer.
- **Many Lives:** Hindus believe in reincarnation, which means that each person has many lives. According to a doctrine called *karma*, what a person does in each life determines what he or she will be in next life. Hindus practice vegetarianism because animals, like people, have a supreme life force.
- **Many Paths to God:** Hindus can connect with God by following his or her own individual path. The caste system is connected to this path. Hindus practice non-violence (including vegetarianism), yoga, and meditation to grow closer to God.

Name _____ Date _____

**CALIFORNIA CONTENT
STANDARD 6.5.3**

# The Roots of Hinduism

**DIRECTIONS: Choose the letter of the *best* answer.**

**1** Karma is the Hindu belief that people's deeds
   **A** should be recorded.
   **B** affect their next life.
   **C** influence animals but not plants.
   **D** are not as important as their prayers.

**2** *One* way Brahmanism evolved into Hinduism was by causing ancient Indians to
   **A** give up eating animals.
   **B** leave their homelands and travel north.
   **C** defeat the Aryans and drive out their gods.
   **D** begin thinking about the origin of the world.

**3** In the early Aryan religion, the ancient sacred Sanskrit texts that recorded rituals and hymns were called the
   **A** Vishnus.
   **B** Mahabharata.
   **C** Vedas.
   **D** Four Noble Truths.

**4** Hinduism includes the belief that the many Hindu deities
   **A** fought each other for power.
   **B** lived together on top of a tall mountain.
   **C** were reborn again and again.
   **D** were all part of one supreme force.

**5** Because Hindus believe that animals share in a supreme life force, many of them
   **A** are afraid of animals.
   **B** worship animals.
   **C** do not eat animals.
   **D** will not touch animals.

**6** The *three* most important Hindu deities are Brahma, the creator, Vishnu, the protector, and Shiva, the
   **A** deity of birth.
   **B** destroyer.
   **C** supreme deity.
   **D** king.

Name _____ Date _____

# The Indian Caste System

**SPECIFIC OBJECTIVE:** Outline the social structure of the caste system.

**Read the summary to answer questions on the next page.**

## The Caste System

- **Developed from Aryans:** Aryans had three classes—warriors, priests, and commoners. Eventually many other groups developed, and the Aryan class system grew into the Hindu caste system.

- **Caste System:** Each caste is a social class whose members are identified by their jobs. Jobs are passed down from father to son. The caste system has thousands of classes, but it is divided into four basic groups.

- **Untouchables:** Later another group developed. Untouchables did the work no one else would do.

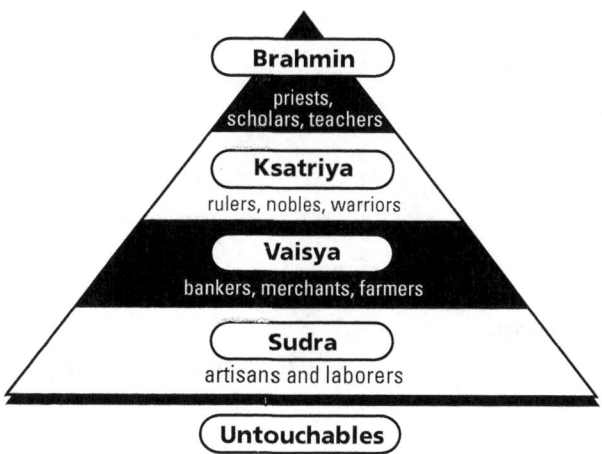

## Four Main Castes

- **Brahmin: the priest caste,** including teachers and scholars, wore white as a symbol of purity. Originally, they performed rituals and sacrifices and needed to be clean for these duties.

- **Ksatriya: the warrior caste,** including nobles and rulers, wore red as a symbol of blood and battle. There were sometimes clashes between the Ksatriya and Brahmana as the priests gained power and popularity.

- **Vaisya: the merchant caste,** including farmers and bankers, wore yellow, the color of turmeric, a common spice used in Indian food.

- **Sudra: the labor caste,** including artisans, wore blue because it was considered the best color for work.

Name _____ Date _____

**PRACTICE**

CALIFORNIA CONTENT
STANDARD 6.5.4

*The Indian Caste System*

**DIRECTIONS: Choose the letter of the *best* answer.**

1  In the Indian caste system, the merchant class wore yellow because it was the color of

   A  the sun.

   B  gold.

   C  the god of trade.

   D  turmeric spice.

2  People's castes in ancient India were determined by

   A  their religions.

   B  their language.

   C  the jobs of their parents.

   D  where they lived.

3  The Brahmin caste in the Hindu culture was named after the

   A  priests in the earlier Aryan religion.

   B  Buddhist god.

   C  jobs they held as warriors.

   D  the color blue they had to wear.

4  In ancient India, if you were someone who made clay pots, you would probably be in which caste?

   A  Brahmin

   B  Ksatriya

   C  Vaisya

   D  Sudra

5  In ancient India, sometimes there were clashes over power between the Ksatriya caste and the

   A  rulers.

   B  Brahmin.

   C  Vaisyas.

   D  Sudras.

6  Where did the Sudras fit in the heirarchy, or levels, of the ancient Indian caste system?

   A  at the top

   B  at the bottom

   C  near the bottom

   D  above the top

Name _____  Date _____

**REVIEW**

CALIFORNIA CONTENT
STANDARD 6.5.5

# *The Spread of Buddhism*

**SPECIFIC OBJECTIVE:** Know the life and moral teachings of Buddha and how Buddhism spread in India, Ceylon, and Central Asia.

**Read the summary below to answer questions on the next page.**

## The Life of Buddha

- **Beginnnings**: Born as Siddhartha Gautama (c. 563 to 483 B.C.), a privileged Hindu prince
- **Changes:** At 29, Siddhartha realized that there was suffering in the world, so he gave up his wealth and went out into world to try to learn the meaning of life.
- **Middle Way:** First, Siddhartha starved himself. In time, he came to believe in the "middle way"—a balance between luxury and self-denial.
- **Buddha:** Siddhartha taught his way of thinking to others. Followers called him Buddha, or "enlightened one." Buddha founded a religion that is known today as Buddhism.

## The Teachings of Buddha

- **The Four Noble Truths:** People suffer because they want things they cannot have. They can stop suffering by following the *Eightfold Path.*
- **The Eightfold Path:** having the right understanding, thought, speech, action, livelihood, effort, mindfulness, and concentration.
- **Nirvana:** Buddha taught that following the Eightfold Path could lead to nirvana, which is the end of all suffering.
- **Buddha and Hinduism:** Like Hindus, Buddhists believed in ahimsa (non-violence). Buddhists do not worship Hindu gods, and they rejected the Hindu caste system.
- **After Buddha's Death:** Followers collected Buddha's teachings, called the *dharma.*

## The Spread of Buddhism

- **In Other Lands:** For a time, Buddhism became widespread in India under King Asoka (299–237 B.C.), who sent Buddhist missionaries to Ceylon (now Sri Lanka). Buddhism eventually spread mainly throughout East Asia and Southeast Asia. It is the major religion today in Burma (now Myanmar), Thailand, China, Laos, Cambodia, Vietnam, Korea, Japan, and Tibet.

**PRACTICE**

CALIFORNIA CONTENT
STANDARD 6.5.5

*The Spread of Buddhism*

---

**DIRECTIONS: Choose the letter of the *best* answer.**

**1** What made Siddhartha Gautama give up his life of privilege as ancient Indian royalty?

  **A** the discovery that there was great suffering in the world

  **B** the lessons he learned from a great teacher

  **C** a priest who told him to help the poor

  **D** his anger at his father

**2** According to Buddhism, what is the "middle way"?

  **A** a collection of his teachings

  **B** a mixture of Hinduism and Buddhism

  **C** a balance between luxury and self-denial

  **D** the career path open to Indians in the middle classes

**3** What is the *dharma* in Buddhism?

  **A** the Indian word for the eightfold path

  **B** the place you reach when you have attained nirvana

  **C** a famous statue of the Buddha

  **D** the teachings of the Buddha collected by his followers

**4** What was the Buddha's relationship to Hinduism?

  **A** Buddha agreed with all the beliefs of Hinduism.

  **B** He did not worship their gods but did believe in ahimsa (non-violence).

  **C** He believed in the caste system, but not the gods and goddesses.

  **D** Buddha rejected everything about Hinduism.

**5** How did King Asoka of India spread Buddhism to Ceylon?

  **A** He defeated Ceylon in war and imposed his religion on them.

  **B** He sent Buddhist missionaries to Ceylon.

  **C** He outlawed the practicing of any other religion.

  **D** He paid the Ceylonese to convert to Buddhism.

**6** What are *three* places where Buddhism spread and became the dominant religion?

  **A** Thailand, Persia, Greece

  **B** Vietnam, Korea, Saudi Arabia

  **C** Laos, Bangladesh, Turkey

  **D** Thailand, Cambodia, Tibet

REVIEW

CALIFORNIA CONTENT
STANDARD 6.5.6

*The Maurya Empire*

**SPECIFIC OBJECTIVE:** Describe the growth of the Maurya empire and the political and moral achievements of the emperor Asoka.

**Read the summary to answer questions on the next page.**

Although Buddhism eventually died out in India, for a time it was the country's most influential religion. This took place under King Asoka (also called Ashoka), a famous king whose grandfather, Chandragupta, built the first Indian empire.

## The Growth of the Maurya Empire

- **A Divided Land:** For several centuries after Buddha lived, India was made up of separate Aryan kingdoms that battled each other for power.
- **Magadha in the Lead:** Around 550 b.c., Magadha, a kingdom in northeastern India, began to grow stronger. In 321 b.c., Chandragupta Maurya became king of the Indian state of Magadha. He went on to conquer much territory and soon controlled most of the Indian subcontinent and parts of present-day Afghanistan.
- **The Maurya Empire:** Chandragupta ruled the first Indian empire.
- **Ruling the Empire:** Chandragupta ruled with spies, his army, and government officials. He taxed the land and people's crops to pay these officials.

## A Buddhist King: Asoka the Great

- **Beginnings:** Grandson of Chandragupta; ruled from around 269 to 232 b.c. Asoka is considered one of the greatest kings in history. sHe crushed a rebellion in the east Indian state of Kalinga, destroyed the city, and killed tens of thousands of men, women, and children.
- **Becoming Buddhist:** Distressed by killing, Asoka decided to try to rule through law, without violence or war. He converted to Buddhism and ruled his kingdom according to Buddhist teachings. Asoka advised people to be truthful and kind, and he urged them to avoid killing.
- **Life in the Empire:** Asoka improved life by fixing roads, planting trees, digging wells and building hospitals and rest houses along the main roads. He sent Buddhist missionaries to neighboring countries and allowed religious freedom in his empire.
- **End of Maurya Empire:** Collapsed only fifty years after Asoka's death. India again became a collection of small kingdoms.

**PRACTICE**

CALIFORNIA CONTENT
STANDARD 6.5.6

# The Maurya Empire

**DIRECTIONS: Choose the letter of the *best* answer.**

**1  The Maurya Empire, which began in ancient India around 550 B.C., was**

  **A**  the longest-lasting empire in Indian history.

  **B**  the last Indian empire.

  **C**  the first Indian empire.

  **D**  the empire that defeated the Indus Valley civilization.

**2  Who was the most *important* king of the Maurya Empire?**

  **A**  Bindusara

  **B**  Asoka

  **C**  Siddhartha Gautama

  **D**  Chandragupta Maurya

**3  What caused Asoka to change the way he ruled India?**

  **A**  a bloody war

  **B**  a religious revelation

  **C**  a sacred promise

  **D**  a military defeat

**4  What was Asoka's policy on religious tolerance in India?**

  **A**  Asoka did not concern himself with religion.

  **B**  Only Buddhism was allowed in the empire.

  **C**  Converts to Buddhism were given special rewards.

  **D**  He allowed religious freedom in the empire.

"Twelve years after my coronation this has been ordered . . . Respect for mother and father is good, generosity to friends, acquaintances, relatives, Brahmans and ascetics is good, not killing living beings is good, moderation in spending and moderation in saving is good."

—from *The Edicts of King Asoka*, translated by Ven S. Dhammika

**5  The inscription shows that King Asoka was concerned with**

  **A**  trading with neighboring states.

  **B**  converting all his people to Buddhism.

  **C**  how people felt about him as a ruler.

  **D**  how people behaved towards each other.

**REVIEW**

CALIFORNIA CONTENT
STANDARD 6.5.7

*India's Legacy*

**SPECIFIC OBJECTIVE:** Discuss important aesthetic and intellectual traditions.

**Read the summary to answer questions on the next page.**

In India, 500 years of disunity followed the end of the Mauryan dynasty. Then, in A.D. 320, Chandra Gupta (who was not related to Chandragupta Maurya) became king. Later his son enlarged the empire by fighting wars. But Chandra Guptas's grandson, Chandra Gupta II, was the greatest ruler of the family. During his reign (A.D. 375–415), India had a Golden Age—a time of peace and prosperity when art and learning flourished.

## Art and Literature

- **Art and Architecture:** Architects built graceful temples. Artists painted murals and sculpted statues, many with religious themes.

- **Drama:** Drama was the greatest literature of the Golden Age. *Shakuntala* is a drama in which a young woman falls in love with a king, who promises to marry her. The king forgets because of a curse laid upon him. *Shakuntala* was written by Kalidasa, who has been compared to Shakespeare.

## Medicine

- **Inoculation:** The first vaccines were given by Indian doctors. Cowpox injections helped stop spread of smallpox. Free hospitals were in use in India 1,000 years before Europe.

- **Surgery:** Doctors sterilized cutting tools, set broken bones, used plastic surgery to fix injured ears and noses, and even performed cataract surgery on eyes.

## Mathematics

- **Number System:** Indians were the first to use a system of numbers based on ten. This system was adopted by the Muslims and passed along to Europe. Indians also invented decimal system and zero (invented independently by the Maya). The Indian numeral system is still in use today.

- **Pi:** identified the value of pi, a measure used to find the circumference and area of any circle.

## Science

- **Metallurgy:** Developed advanced methods of metallurgy (metal working). Metal workers built an iron pillar in Delhi that towers almost 23 feet high. The tower has resisted rust for sixteen centuries.

**PRACTICE**

**CALIFORNIA CONTENT STANDARD 6.5.7**

*India's Legacy*

**DIRECTIONS: Choose the letter of the *best* answer.**

**1** During Indian's Golden Age, what was the name of the most famous playwright?

**A** Shakuntala

**B** Ayurvedic

**C** Kalidasa

**D** Chandra Gupta II

**2** Hospitals during India's Golden Age differed from other hospitals of the time in that they were

**A** spotlessly clean.

**B** run by certified doctors.

**C** free to the public.

**D** open to the upper class only.

**3** What important mathematical idea was invented independently by the Maya and in India?

**A** geometry

**B** algebra

**C** square roots

**D** concept of zero

**4** What concept helped mathematicians in ancient India find the area and circumference of any circle?

**A** pi

**B** decimals

**C** rulers

**D** exact measurements

**5** What medical procedure, common today, was performed in ancient India?

**A** back surgery

**B** cataract surgery

**C** appendectomy

**D** heart transplant

**6** A tall metal column free of rust stands today in the Indian city of Delhi due to ancient Indian developments in

**A** metallurgy.

**B** ayurvedic.

**C** mathematics.

**D** weights and measures.

Name _____ Date _____

# Origins of Chinese Civilization

**SPECIFIC OBJECTIVE:** Locate and describe the origins of Chinese civilization in the Huang-He valley during the Shang dynasty.

**Read the summary and chart to answer questions on the next page.**

The walls of China's first cities were built 1,500 years after the walls of Sumer; 1,000 years after the great pyramids of Egypt; and 1,000 years after the cities of the Indus Valley. The civilization, begun on China's Huang He River 3,500 years ago, outlasted all the others. It continues into the 21st century.

| The Huang He River Valley |
|---|
| • **Geography:** The Huang He River is a long, twisting river that flows out of the highlands of Tibet. The river flows east until it reaches a broad, flat pocket of land near the Pacific Ocean. This broad plain is cupped on the north, west, and south by hills and mountains. About 90 percent of China's farmland lies in this small region. |
| • **The Yellow River:** The Huang He is also called the "Yellow" River because the river's color is yellow. From the western mountains, the water picks up a dusty yellow soil called *loess*. The river spreads the loess over farming fields. Winds from the west bring more rich loess that keeps the farmland of China fertile. |
| • **China's Sorrow:** The Huang He River is unpredictable. Its floods can be generous or ruinous. At its worst, the river devours whole villages. The river has been nicknamed "China's Sorrow." Yet, the rich farmland constantly draws people back to the river valley. |

| The Shang Dynasty |
|---|
| • **China's First Cities:** About 2000 B.C., farming settlements along the Huang He began to grow into cities. Among the oldest and most important cities was Anyang. |
| • **Shang Kings:** About 1766 B.C., Shang family kings began to control some cities. They set up a dynasty, or rule by generations of one family. Shang kings were responsible for religious activities. They also claimed to rule with the gods' permission. Shang kings controlled the central portion of the North China Plain. They often made war with nomadic people such as the Zhou. Shang kings are thought to have ruled from 1766 B.C. to 1027 B.C. |
| • **Family Ties:** In Shang culture, respect for parents and ancestors was important. The family was closely linked to religion. The spirits of family ancestors were thought to have the power to bring good fortune or disaster. Families paid respect to the father's ancestors by making animal sacrifices to the gods. Men ruled the family. Women were treated as inferiors. |
| • **Writing:** Chinese writing developed through religious practices. It used pictographs, stylized symbol-drawing called characters, for words or ideas. An educated person at the time knew more than 10,000 characters. |

PRACTICE

CALIFORNIA CONTENT
STANDARD 6.6.1

# Origins of Chinese Civilization

**DIRECTIONS: Choose the letter of the *best* answer.**

**Use the map to answer questions 1 and 2.**

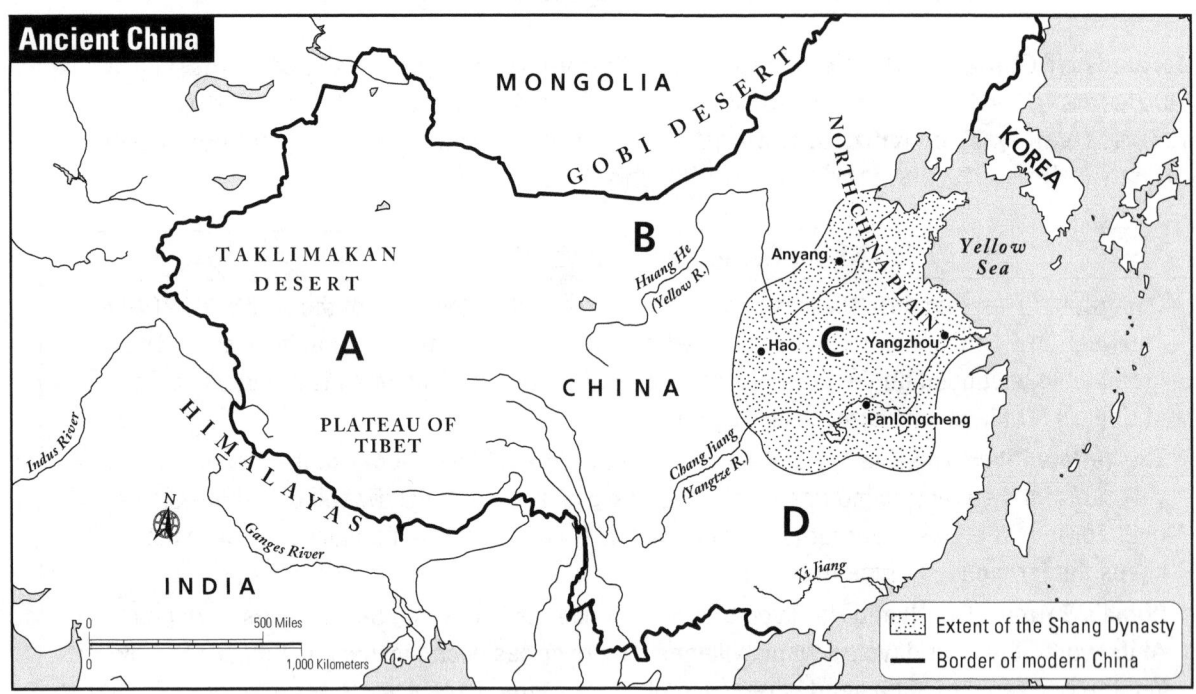

**Ancient China**

MONGOLIA

GOBI DESERT

TAKLIMAKAN
DESERT

A

PLATEAU OF
TIBET

HIMALAYAS

Indus River

Ganges River

INDIA

CHINA

Huang He
(Yellow R.)

B

Hao

Chang Jiang
(Yangtze R.)

Xi Jiang

NORTH CHINA PLAIN

Anyang

C

Yangzhou

Panlongcheng

D

KOREA

Yellow
Sea

N

0           500 Miles
0        1,000 Kilometers

⬚ Extent of the Shang Dynasty
— Border of modern China

**1** Which area on the map was the site of the earliest farming settlements in China?

  **A**  Area *A*

  **B**  Area *B*

  **C**  Area *C*

  **D**  Area *D*

**2** Anyang was one of the capitals of the Shang Dynasty. Describe its location on the map.

  **A**  on the Xi Jiang in southern China

  **B**  on the Yangtze, near Yangzhou

  **C**  on the Yangtze, near the Plateau of Tibet

  **D**  near the Huang He, on the North China Plain

Name _____   Date _____

**REVIEW**

CALIFORNIA CONTENT
STANDARD 6.6.2

# The Geography of
# Ancient China

**SPECIFIC OBJECTIVE:** Explain the geographic features of China that
made governance and the spread of ideas and goods difficult and
served to isolate the country from the rest of the world.

**Read the sequence diagram to answer questions on the next page.**

| Geographic Features |
|---|
| • Ancient China's geography isolated it from other civilizations.<br>• To its east lay the Pacific Ocean.<br>• To the west lay the forbidding Taklimakan Desert and the icy 14,000-foot Plateau of Tibet.<br>• To the southwest were the towering Himalayas.<br>• To the north lived the warlike nomads of Mongolia and the endless Gobi Desert.<br>• In ancient times, most Chinese farming was done in the land between the Yangtze in central China and the Huang He in northern China. This land, called the North China Plain, has always been the center of Chinese civilization. |

↓

| Climate |
|---|
| • China has a varied climate like the United States.<br>• Western China is dry like the American West.<br>• Northern China has seasons like New England. Here, in the colder and drier North, the Chinese grow wheat and millet.<br>• The southeastern part of China is warm and moist. This climate is ideal for growing rice. |

↓

| The Middle Kingdom |
|---|
| In the Chinese view, only barbarians (people who are not civilized) lived outside China's borders. Because the Chinese saw their country as the center of the civilized world, their own name for China was the Middle Kingdom. The ancient Chinese people generally had no need to interact with other cultures or civilizations. |

Name _____     Date _____

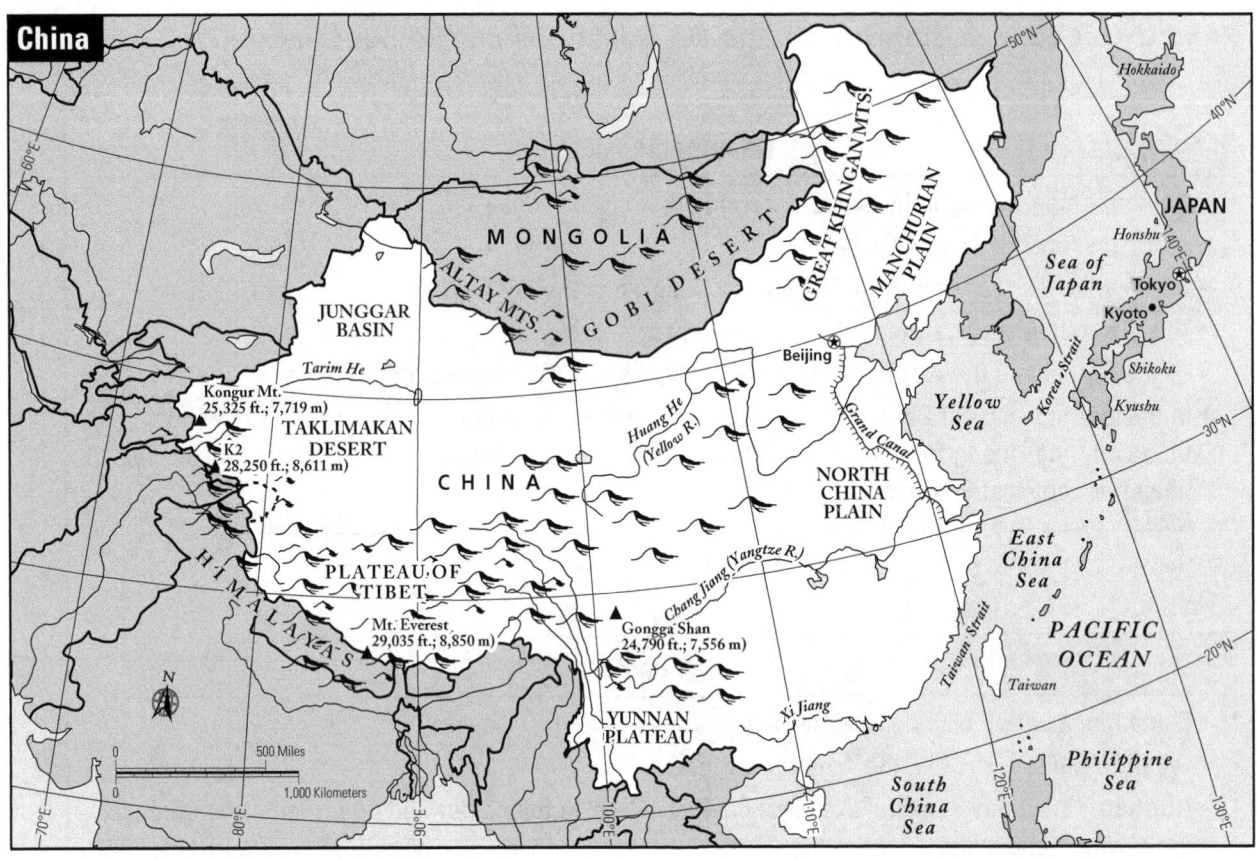

# The Geography of Ancient China

---

**DIRECTIONS: Choose the letter of the *best* answer.**

**Use the map to answer questions 1 and 2.**

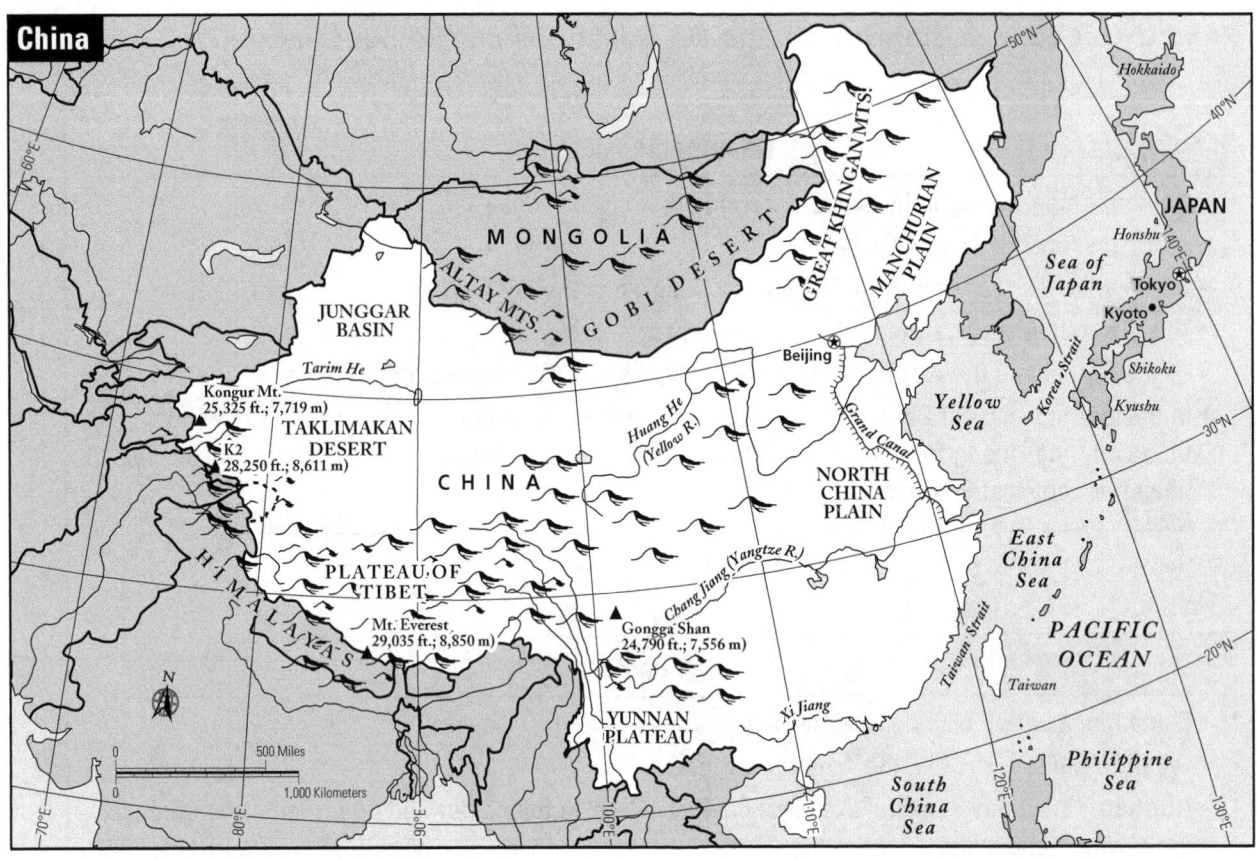

**1** The Himalaya Mountains and the Plateau of Tibet border the North China Plain on the

**A** northeast.

**B** east.

**C** south.

**D** southwest.

**2** If travelers in ancient times wanted to reach the civilizations of China from the west, they would have to cross the

**A** Taklimakan Desert.

**B** Gobi Desert.

**C** Xi Jiang River.

**D** Yellow Sea.

**REVIEW**

**CALIFORNIA CONTENT
STANDARD 6.6.3**

*Confucianism and Taoism*

**SPECIFIC OBJECTIVE:** Know about the life of Confucius and the fundamental teachings of Confucianism and Taoism.

**Read the summary and chart to answer questions on the next page.**

After 800 B.C., nomads from the north and west invaded China. Invaders destroyed China's capital and killed the king. The royal family escaped to Luoyang and set up a new capital. Because the kings were weak, the lords fought constantly. Scholars wondered what it would take to bring peace. Over time, new beliefs developed, including Confucianism and Taoism.

| The Life of Confucius (551–479 B.C.) | Basic Teachings of Confucianism | Basic Teachings of Taoism |
|---|---|---|
| • Born into a poor family<br>• Great unrest and conflict in China during his life<br>• Spent most of his life as a teacher of children and of people who admired him<br>• Wanted to make society peaceful and just<br>• Appointed Minister of Justice in his home state at about age 50<br>• Legends say he did such a good job and his town was so free of crime that a lost purse would not be touched for days.<br>• Later, he lost support of the rulers and lost his job as a minister.<br>• He continued his teachings but felt he was a failure because he did not hold a high office. | • After Confucius's death, his teachings were passed down through the years and were collected in *The Analects.*<br>• Focused on proper behavior (propriety) in relationships; people should respect each other at all times.<br>• **Five basic relationships:**<br>• *Family relationships—* **between parent and child; elder and younger; husband and wife.**<br>• *Social relationships—* **between friend and friend;** and **ruler and subject.**<br>• Rulers should be a living example of a good life.<br>• One should have respect for one's parents. | • Legend says Taoism was founded by **Laozi** in 500s B.C.<br>• **"Tao" or the Way— a universal force that guides all things.**<br>• All creatures, except humans, live in harmony with this force.<br>• A human must seek his or her own personal *tao*, or "way" to live in harmony with nature; there are no simple rules to follow.<br>• Followers did not need to debate good and bad or try to change things; they must accept opposing forces.<br>• Followers did not want to be in government.<br>• Teachings contrasted sharply with Confucianism. |

**PRACTICE**

CALIFORNIA CONTENT
STANDARD 6.6.3

## Confucianism and Taoism

---

**DIRECTIONS: Choose the letter of the *best* answer.**

**1** Confucius was born

  **A** into a family of nobles who allowed him to study constantly.

  **B** during a time of peace and prosperity in China.

  **C** in Japan and traveled to China later.

  **D** into a poor family during a time of conflict in China.

**2** Legends say that when Confucius was the minister of justice,

  **A** he supported the execution of any thieves.

  **B** he abolished courts and became the only judge.

  **C** crime and corruption was eliminated in his town.

  **D** a strong army volunteered to help him enforce order.

**3** Confucianism says that in all relationships, people should use

  **A** proper behavior.

  **B** prayer for inspiration.

  **C** government laws to guide them.

  **D** no simple rules, but harmony with nature.

**4** Confucius taught the importance of five special relationships, including

  **A** business partnership.

  **B** ruler and subject.

  **C** humans and nature.

  **D** the fellowship of teams.

**5** What did Taoists believe about the Tao and nature?

  **A** Animals and humans are the same.

  **B** Humans must seek harmony with nature.

  **C** Nature has a Tao that must be tamed by humans.

  **D** Humans can never find harmony in nature.

**6** In general, what did Taoists feel about change?

  **A** Change always makes things better, so it is good.

  **B** People should not struggle to change things, but simply accept them.

  **C** Change is only good if you are trying to change laws or government.

  **D** If a ruler would change for the better, everyone's life would improve.

**REVIEW**

**CALIFORNIA CONTENT
STANDARD 6.6.4**

## Problems in China in the Time of Confucius

**SPECIFIC OBJECTIVE:** Identify the political and cultural problems prevalent in the time of Confucius and how he sought to solve them.

**Read the summary and chart to answer questions on the next page.**

The Zhou people moved down from the northwest. They clashed with the Shang many times. Around 1027 B.C., the Zhou ruler Wu Wang led a force that defeated the Shang. A new dynasty had come to power in ancient China.

| Political and Cultural Problems in China (about 550–480 B.C.) | Confucius's Approach |
|---|---|
| **Political Problems**<br>• **Mandate of Heaven:** Just ruler had divine approval. Wicked leader could lose divine approval; applied to Zhou dynasty.<br>• Local leaders were corrupt and unfair.<br>• There was constant political conflict.<br>• Relationships between leaders and people remained always uncertain.<br>• The Zhou dynasty's weakness led to inability to fight off invasion in 771 B.C.<br>• Zhou dynasty continued to rule, but local lords challenged Zhou kings.<br>• Known as the "Time of the Warring States"<br><br>**Social Problems**<br>• Traditional values collapsed.<br>• Chaos, arrogance, and defiance replaced love of order, harmony, and respect for authority.<br>• As cities grew, crime increased.<br>• Education became less important. | **Political Problems**<br>• Stressed that there was a proper relationship between rulers and subjects:<br>• Rulers should set an example by leading a good life.<br>• Rulers should treat subjects with respect.<br>• If a ruler used proper behavior and showed respect to his people, then the subject's responsibility was to obey the ruler's laws and commands.<br>• If rulers and subjects followed these rules, society would be peaceful.<br><br>**Social Problems**<br>1) Stressed proper relationships among family members and among members of society:<br>  • "What you do not want done to yourself, do not do to others."<br>  • A peaceful family should have clear roles that focus on respect.<br>  • Wives should obey husbands.<br>  • Younger children should obey elders.<br>  • Families should respect ancestors.<br>2) Stressed education as a form of individual improvement |

**PRACTICE**

CALIFORNIA CONTENT
STANDARD 6.6.4

# Problems in China in the Time of Confucius

**DIRECTIONS: Choose the letter of the *best* answer.**

**1** During Confucius's lifetime (551–479 B.C.), lords and kings

  **A** cooperated to form a stable national government.

  **B** belonged to the same royal family.

  **C** fought each other for control.

  **D** used the same large army to enforce order.

**2** Because of the Mandate of Heaven, the Chinese people believed a famine or flood was a sign that

  **A** the king was very powerful.

  **B** the king had lost the approval of the gods.

  **C** the next year would be better.

  **D** there had been climate changes.

**3** What was one factor that caused the Zhou dynasty's loss of power?

  **A** great floods and earthquakes

  **B** an invasion by "barbarians" in 771 B.C.

  **C** loss of respect between kings and nobles

  **D** an increase in population

**4** Confucius taught that rulers should

  **A** be chosen by their subjects according to their abilities.

  **B** consult with their subjects before making any decisions.

  **C** be paid no more than the best workmen.

  **D** set an example for their subjects by leading a good life.

**5** Which rule did Confucius feel should guide people's actions?

  **A** "Turn the other cheek."

  **B** "What you do not want done to yourself, do not do to others."

  **C** "Only respect those that respect you."

  **D** "Everyone belongs to the same family, and all are equal."

**6** As *one* solution to social problems, Confucius thought that education

  **A** was an important way for people to improve themselves.

  **B** should be offered to the children of rulers.

  **C** was important for those entering into business.

  **D** could be a useful way to focus on Confucius's writings.

**REVIEW**

CALIFORNIA CONTENT
STANDARD 6.6.5

## Achievements During the Qin Dynasty

**SPECIFIC OBJECTIVE:** List the policies and achievements of the emperor Shi Huangdi in unifying northern China under the Qin Dynasty.

**Read the summary and chart to answer questions on the next page.**

At the end of the Zhou period, several states were still at war. According to the Mandate of Heaven, war was a sign that the ruling dynasty had lost heaven's favor. A new ruler was needed. That ruler would be Shi Huangdi, and he did what no other ruler before him had been able to do. In 221 B.C., Shi Huangdi united all of China's kingdoms, or states.

| Policies of Shi Huangdi | Achievements (221–202 B.C.) |
|---|---|
| • At 13 years of age, in 256 B.C., he ruled the state of Qin.<br>• As he grew older, he became a ruthless leader.<br>• In 221 B.C., he took the name Shi Huangdi, which means "First Emperor," a title previously used only for gods.<br>• **Uniting China:** He conquered neighboring states.<br>• To install a strong central government, he weakened defeated nobles by taking their land.<br>• Forced nobles to live at capital, so he could watch them<br>• **Believed in Legalism**—people needed to be forced by government to live correctly and be punished harshly if they did not obey government laws<br>• Tried to erase Confucianism by killing believers and burning Confucian books<br>• Forced peasants to work on large government projects (Great Wall, highways, irrigation projects). Many died from overwork and poor working conditions.<br>• Collected high taxes to pay for projects | • Unified China under one government<br>• Expanded Chinese territory<br>• Employed thousands of soldiers to keep borders safe and maintain peace in China<br>• Began work on Great Wall for protection from north; work continued over many years, linked smaller walls that had been built earlier. The Great Wall has been built, rebuilt, and extended many times.<br>• United country with highways and irrigation projects—made trade and farming easier<br>• Hired thousands of officials to keep canals and roads repaired and collect taxes<br>• Officials made sure that even the smallest village knew the laws.<br>• Set government standards for weights, measures, coins, and writing that made business and trade easier |

Name _____ Date _____

PRACTICE

**CALIFORNIA CONTENT
STANDARD 6.6.5**

# Achievements During
# the Qin Dynasty

---

**DIRECTIONS: Choose the letter of the *best* answer.**

**Use the map to answer questions 1 and 2.**

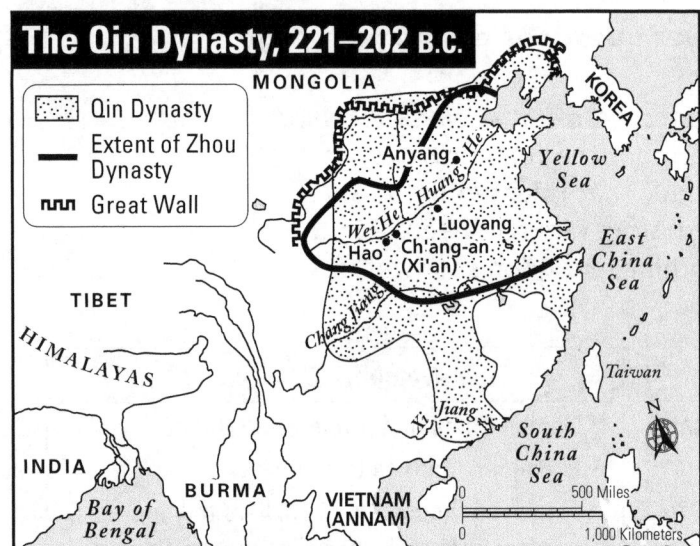

**1** According to the map, how do the Zhou Dynasty and the Qin dynasty under Shi Huangdi compare?

  **A** The extent of the Zhou dynasty reaches to the South China Sea.

  **B** The Qin Dynasty includes the territory ruled by the Zhou.

  **C** Both empires are roughly equal in territory.

  **D** The Qin Dynasty controlled more land in the west; the Zhou Dynasty, more in the south.

**2** According to the map, the Great Wall protected China from invaders from

  **A** Tibet.

  **B** Burma.

  **C** Mongolia.

  **D** Vietnam.

**3** During the Qin dynasty, peasants

  **A** were forced to work on government projects, like highways and the Great Wall.

  **B** were given control of their own villages.

  **C** were allowed to collect taxes from wealthy landowners.

  **D** were rewarded for helping Shi Huangdi conquer new lands.

**4** During the Qin dynasty, trade and business became easier because

  **A** the government forced neighbor countries to allow traders in.

  **B** silk was invented and used to trade with other countries.

  **C** ports on the Yellow Sea were opened.

  **D** the government set standards for coins, weights, and measures.

Copyright © McDougal Littell/Houghton Mifflin Company

**88** CSS Specific Objective 6.6.5: Practice

**CALIFORNIA CONTENT STANDARD 6.6.6**

# The Han Dynasty

**SPECIFIC OBJECTIVE:** Detail the political contributions of the Han Dynasty to the development of the imperial bureaucratic state and the expansion of the empire.

**Read the summary and chart to answer questions on the next page.**

The First Emperor had dreamed his family would rule China for 10,000 generations. It did not. Shi Huangdi had not set a good example. His son was even less effective. Eventually, a military general named Liu Bang defeated Qin forces. In 202 B.C., he started the Han Dynasty. The Chinese think of the Han years as a time of glory, peace, and unity. It would last until 220 A.D., during the same time period as the Roman Empire.

| The Han Dynasty 202 B.C.–A.D. 220 |
|---|
| **Government** |
| • Strong central government continued but with lower taxes and milder punishments. |
| • Peasants were still required to work on government projects such as roads, canals, and irrigation projects, but for only one month per year. |
| • Began government bureaucracy, in which officials chosen by the ruler ran offices, or bureaus. The officials help enforce the leader's rule. |
| • People who passed tests on Confucius's writing were chosen for high government positions. Soon, the most powerful officials were scholars who had mastered Confucianism. |
| **Expanding the Empire** |
| • The most powerful of the Han emperors was Wudi (140–87 B.C.). |
| • Known as the Martial Emperor because of success in battle |
| • Han armies struck up to 2,000 miles from emperor's palace. |
| • Extended boundaries of empire mostly to the south (southern Chinese provinces; northern Vietnam) and west (central Asia) but also to the northeast to include what is now northern Korea |
| • Drove back northern Barbarians, the Huns, beyond the Great Wall |
| **Daily Life** |
| • Wudi made Confucianism the official set of beliefs for his government. |
| • Most people were farmers, living in villages with mud houses and using simple farming tools. |
| • Farmers in the cool north grew wheat or millet. In the warmer south, they grew rice. |
| • Fish and meat were available, but expensive. As a result, most people ate small portions of meat and fish. |
| • Many people also lived in crowded, exciting cities. Cities were centers for trade, education, government, merchants, and artisans. |

Name _____    Date _____

**DIRECTIONS: Choose the letter of the *best* answer.**

**Use the map to answer questions 1 and 2.**

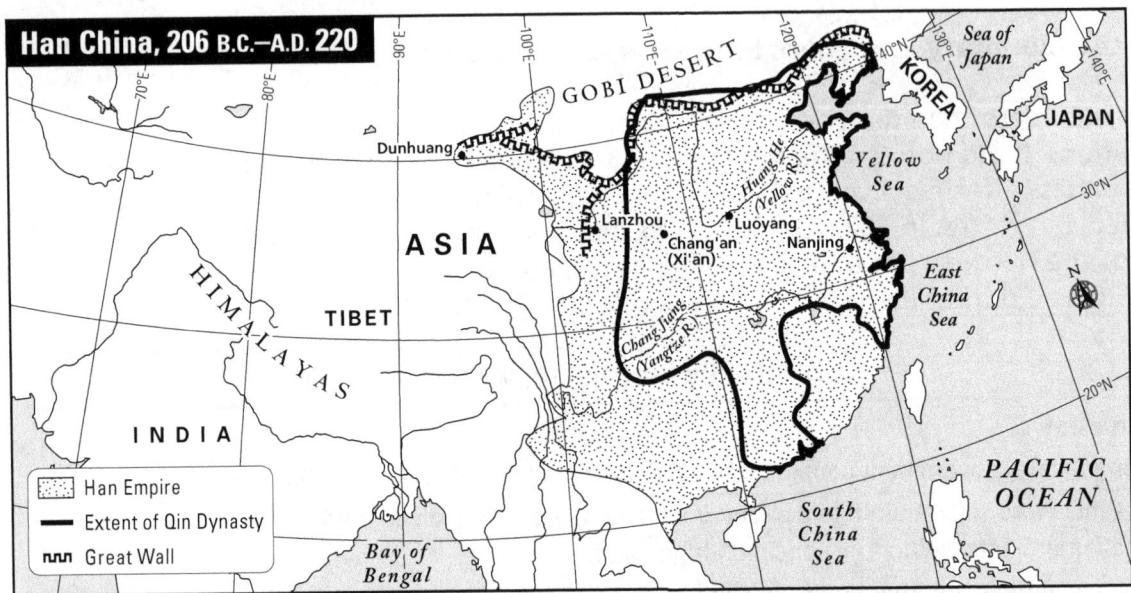

**Han China, 206 B.C.–A.D. 220**

GOBI DESERT

Sea of Japan

KOREA

JAPAN

Dunhuang

Huang He (Yellow R.)

Yellow Sea

ASIA

Lanzhou

Luoyang

Chang'an (Xi'an)

Nanjing

East China Sea

HIMALAYAS

TIBET

Chang Jiang (Yangtze R.)

INDIA

Han Empire
Extent of Qin Dynasty
Great Wall

Bay of Bengal

South China Sea

PACIFIC OCEAN

**1** In which direction did China add the most territory during the Han Dynasty?

**A** north and south

**B** west

**C** south and east

**D** east

**2** In which direction did China extend the Great Wall the farthest during the Han Dynasty?

**A** north

**B** west

**C** south

**D** east

**3** What is **one** way the Han Dynasty changed policies of the Qin Dynasty?

**A** Peasants worked one month per year on government projects.

**B** The central government became weaker, because local governments became stronger.

**C** Punishments for opposing the government became harsher.

**D** Nobles were given power to raise their own local armies.

**4** In general, the Han Dynasty in China was a time of

**A** power and prosperity.

**B** political conflict.

**C** religious wars.

**D** economic depression and hardship.

**REVIEW**

**CALIFORNIA CONTENT STANDARD 6.6.7**

## The Silk Roads

**SPECIFIC OBJECTIVE:** Cite the significance of the trans-Eurasian "silk roads" in the period of the Han Dynasty and Roman Empire and their locations.

**Read the summary to answer questions on the next page.**

During the time of the Han Dynasty, only the Chinese knew how to make silk. It was much desired as a luxury fabric both by the people of China and outsiders. In fact, it was silk that first linked China with Southwest Asia and the rest of the civilized world.

### The Silk Roads

- Overland trade routes were called Silk Roads because traders carried silk and other goods on camel caravans.
- Trade from China became common by about 100 B.C.
- The trails stretched westward from China, through Central Asia to Southwest Asia, and across the Mediterranean by ship to the Roman Empire in Europe. Trails were often called Trans-Eurasian because they stretched across two continents—Europe and Asia.
- Chinese traders began at Ch'ang-an and went as far as Kashgar in Central Asia where they traded with central Asian nomads. At Dunhuang, the trail split to avoid the harsh Taklimakan Desert. The trail also split to avoid mountains and harsh weather.
- After a journey of 4,000 miles, Chinese silk and other goods from China reached the markets of Antioch and Damascus in Southwest Asia. By that time, silk had changed hands many times, each time for a higher price.
- Goods from Rome traveled east along the same trails to China.

### Trading Goods and Ideas

- Trade goods needed to be of very high value and light so they were worth transporting thousands of miles by camel and ship.
- The Chinese traded silk (which they alone knew how to make), paper (another Chinese invention), and pottery.
- Goods from the west to China included sesame seeds and oil, gold and silver, precious stones, and central Asian horses.
- People in Europe were affected by Chinese and other Asian cultures. At the same time the Chinese were affected by western influences in religion, art, and military methods.

**PRACTICE**

**CALIFORNIA CONTENT STANDARD 6.6.7**

*The Silk Roads*

**DIRECTIONS: Choose the letter of the *best* answer.**

**Use the map to answer questions 1 and 2.**

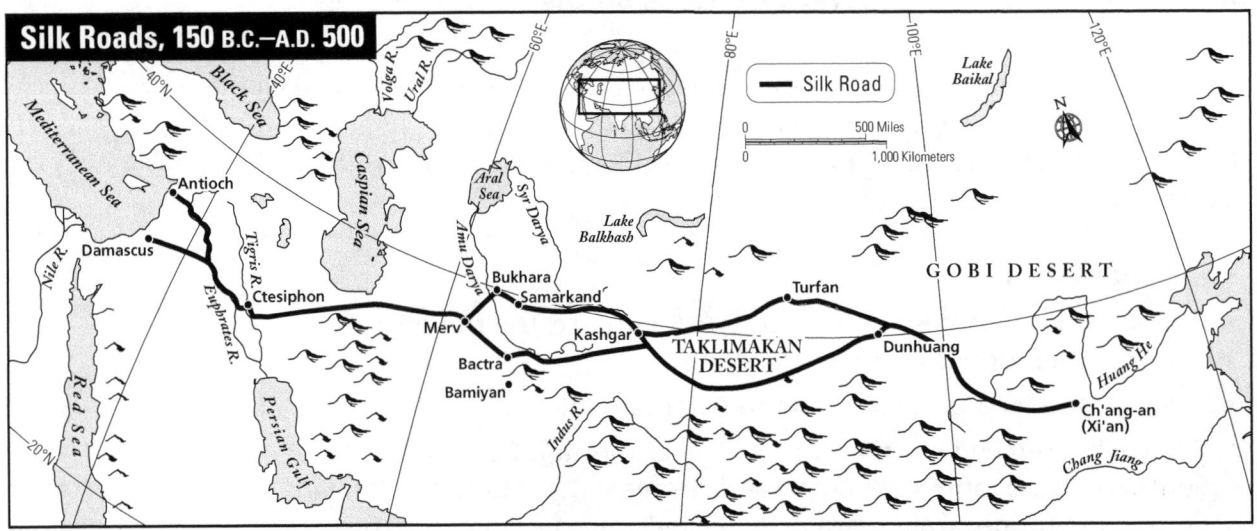

Silk Roads, 150 B.C.–A.D. 500

1   Between which *two* cities did the trail of silk travel without branching off or splitting?

   A   Ch'ang-an and Kashgar.

   B   Kashgar and Merv.

   C   Merv and Ctesiphon.

   D   Ctesiphon and Rome.

2   The *main* route of the Silk Roads split between Dunhuang and Kashgar in order to

   A   go around the Himalayas.

   B   avoid the Taklimakan Desert.

   C   avoid the Gobi Desert.

   D   by-pass fierce nomads from central Asia.

3   On the Silk Roads, Chinese traders usually traded for

   A   paper, pottery, and tea.

   B   Central Asian horses, gold, and oil.

   C   Southwest Asian spices, methods of dressing, and food.

   D   Roman coins, military tactics, and murals.

4   Influences from trade along the Silk Roads caused changes in China's

   A   transportation.

   B   agriculture.

   C   government and constitution.

   D   art, religion, and military methods.

Name _____    Date _____

**REVIEW**

**CALIFORNIA CONTENT
STANDARD 6.6.8**

# Buddhism Moves into China

---

**SPECIFIC OBJECTIVE:** Describe the diffusion of Buddhism northward
into China during the Han Dynasty.

**Read the summary and chart to answer questions on the next page.**

In the years following Wudi's reign, Chinese prosperity declined. Chinese peasants
suffered most in any time of trouble. They lived under a crushing burden of debts
and taxes. In the last years of Han reign, cruel and corrupt officials gained power.
The people of China were ready for a change.

| Buddhism Moves into China |
|---|
| • During the late years of the Han Dynasty, between 50 B.C. and A.D. 100, Buddhism became increasingly popular in China. |
| • Buddhism came to China with traders and missionaries on the Silk Road or on trade vessels from the Indian Ocean. |
| • In the villages of China, Buddhist monks taught that Buddha had been a merciful god who came to earth to save human souls. |

| Buddhism Becomes More Popular |
|---|
| • Worship of family ancestors continued in China, but people were also eager to embrace new beliefs. Millions of Chinese turned to the kindly Buddha. |
| • Unlike Confucius, who taught that humans should strive for a better life, Buddhism taught that suffering was part of life. This belief helped a society with social problems and conflict. |
| • Although Buddha, now dead for five centuries, had never claimed to be a god, people in China began carving statues to him. In the rocky cliffs of northern China, huge statues of Buddha were carved into sandstone cliffs. One such Buddha measured 50 feet from top to bottom. |
| • By A.D.100, Buddhist monks had established temples to Buddha. |

| China Changes Buddhism |
|---|
| • As Buddhism became more popular in China, people changed it to fit in better with Chinese beliefs. |
| • Even when people became Buddhists, they might also continue to follow Confucianism and Taoism (or Daoism). |
| • Chinese Buddhists of the time made Buddha part of the family of Chinese gods. |
| • There were Chinese gods for planets, war, earth, and rain. Now Buddha became one of these gods (along with other good people who had lived on Earth). |

**PRACTICE**

**CALIFORNIA CONTENT STANDARD 6.6.8**

# Buddhism Moves into China

**DIRECTIONS: Choose the letter of the *best* answer.**

1  The end of the Han Dynasty around 50 B.C. was marked by
   A  continued prosperity.
   B  corrupt officials, high taxes, and misery.
   C  a renewal of an interest in Confucianism.
   D  the rise of a new emperor who promised peace.

2  Buddhism was first brought to China by
   A  soldiers.
   B  trading ships.
   C  traders and missionaries.
   D  the Great Wall.

3  The movement of Buddhism into China was made easier by
   A  the Silk Roads.
   B  the invention of sailing ships.
   C  the development of standard Chinese writing.
   D  the Great Wall.

4  Buddhism was different from Confucianism because it taught that
   A  people will not be reborn into another life.
   B  suffering is part of life.
   C  people should strive for a stable society.
   D  emperors were not descended from the gods.

5  When Buddhism first appeared in China, Buddha was looked upon as a
   A  hero.
   B  prosperous ruler.
   C  wise man.
   D  god.

6  With the arrival of Buddhism, how did the Chinese view their family ancestors?
   A  They no longer believed in them.
   B  They continued to worship them.
   C  They thought Buddhism was more important.
   D  They began carving statues of them.

Name _____     Date _____

# Rise of the Roman Republic

**SPECIFIC OBJECTIVE:** Identify the location and describe the rise of the Roman Republic, including the importance of such mythical and historical figures as Aeneas, Romulus and Remus, Cincinnatus, Julius Caesar, and Cicero.

**Read the summary and map to answer questions on the next page.**

Italy is a **peninsula,** west of Greece. It borders the **Mediterranean Sea** and has a mild climate. Among the many early groups living in Italy were the **Latins.** On a hill, overlooking a large, fertile plain, a few Latin shepherds built a village. That village would one day rule not only Italy but also much of Europe, Asia, and North Africa.

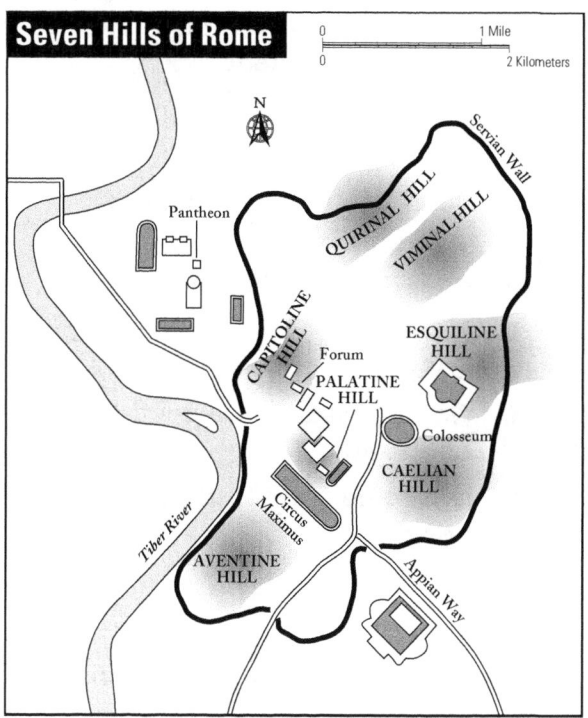

## Hills, Rivers, and the Sea

- Rome began as a cluster of huts atop the 300-foot **Palatine Hill,** one of seven steep hills on the **Tiber River** in central Italy.
- A fertile plain, good for farming, lay at the base of the hills. The Tiber provided water.
- Italy's location on the Mediterranean Sea made it easy for Roman ships to reach other lands and trade. The Tiber gave Romans access to the Mediterranean.

## Important Figures in the Roman Republic

- **Aeneas,** one of the Trojan warriors in Homer's *Iliad,* having been told he would found a great city, finally settled a region called Latium along the Tiber River.
- **Romulus and Remus,** said to be descendants of Aeneas, were twins who, according to legend, were abandoned by their mother, rescued by a wolf, and raised by a shepherd.
- **Cincinnatus,** a Roman consul in 460 B.C. became a legendary hero. During two wars, the citizens made him dictator, or total ruler, for a limited time. Cincinnatus left his beloved farm and saved Rome. Afterwards, offered a gold crown and the title of king, he instead returned to his farm.
- **Julius Caesar** was another military hero, who won popular support. In 46 B.C., the Senate made him sole Roman ruler. Two years later, he made himself dictator for life, and, in the same year, was assassinated.
- **Cicero** was a key Roman consul and perhaps the greatest public speaker in Roman history. He spoke out against Caesar's quest for power.

Name _____   Date _____

# *Rise of the Roman Republic*

**DIRECTIONS: Choose the letter of the *best* answer.**

1  The Latins first settled on seven hills in central Italy overlooking a plain that

   A  was excellent for farming.

   B  bordered the ocean.

   C  offered protection from attack.

   D  was thickly covered with forest.

2  What is the name of the body of water on which Rome is located?

   A  the Mediterranean Sea

   B  the Tiber River

   C  the Aegean Sea

   D  the Tigris River

3  According to legend, Romulus and Remus were

   A  twin wolf cubs.

   B  raised by their father.

   C  half-brothers, born to different mothers.

   D  descendants of Aeneas.

4  How did Cincinnatus exemplify the traits that early Romans most admired?

   A  He was offered a gold crown but preffered to live a simple life.

   B  He made himself dictator for life.

   C  He ruled as a kind and caring king.

   D  He allowed all citizens to have a say in government.

5  In 44 B.C., after making himself dictator for life, Julius Caesar

   A  retired from office as consul.

   B  wrote famous speeches against expanding the empire.

   C  was assassinated by political opponents.

   D  left Rome and returned to his home in Gaul.

6  Cicero, who lived during the time of Caesar, was

   A  a businessman who was never elected to office.

   B  a great speaker who strongly supported the republic.

   C  a judge who ruled against Julius Caesar.

   D  a designer of Roman walls and roads.

**REVIEW**

**CALIFORNIA CONTENT STANDARD 6.7.2**

*Government of the Roman Republic*

**SPECIFIC OBJECTIVE:** Describe the government of the Roman Republic and its significance.

**Read the summary and chart to answer questions on the next page.**

As trade in ancient times grew, neighboring people became jealous of the Latin villages. One such group, the Etruscans, took over the seven Latin villages. The Etruscan kings built roads and fine houses, but the Latins rebelled. In 509 B.C.., the Latins drove out the last Etruscan king and set up a republic, a government ruled by a temporary elected group.

| Government Structure |
|---|
| • **Twelve Tables:** In 450 B.C., the laws of the Republic, carved on twelve stone tablets, hung in public for everyone to see. It established the idea that all citizens had a right to equal protection. |
| • **Tripartite Government:** Three separate parts to the government: |
|    1. **Legislative Branch:** Made laws; included a senate of wealthy landowners, known as patricians. Patricians advised leaders. Also included assemblies of common people called plebeians who protected rights of commoners. |
|    2. **Judicial Branch:** Eight judges to oversee courts and govern provinces. |
|    3. **Executive Branch:** Two elected consuls for one year. Each had veto power, which meant that one consul could not do anything without the approval of the other. |
| • **Dictator:** In a time of crisis, such as war, consuls could appoint a temporary dictator. |
| • **Not Direct Democracy:** Although Rome was a republic, it was not a direct democracy. In a direct democracy, all citizens participate in government. In the Roman Republic, participation was given over to elected representatives. In addition, the right to vote was limited to free adult males. |

**Roman and Other Republics** The government of the United States has many features in common with the early Roman Republic:

• Both have **three branches** of government.

• Both have **leaders that are elected** rather than passed down in families.

• Both have **two parts of the legislative branch:** an upper house and a lower house.

**PRACTICE**

CALIFORNIA CONTENT
STANDARD 6.7.2

# Government of the Roman Republic

---

**DIRECTIONS: Choose the letter of the *best* answer.**

**1** The Twelve Tables were

  **A** the place where patricians met within the Senate.

  **B** the laws of the Republic that were displayed in public.

  **C** the system used for determining prices in the market.

  **D** instructions to plebeians that limited their rights.

**2** What was the make up of Rome's legislative branch?

  **A** two consuls elected by the people

  **B** the Senate and the judicial branch

  **C** a Senate of patricians and assemblies of plebeians

  **D** a dictator chosen for life

**3** The executive branch of the Roman Republic was composed of two elected consuls. Both consuls had veto power and were

  **A** elected for one year.

  **B** appointed by the judges for life.

  **C** thought to be descended from Roman gods.

  **D** representatives of Roman provinces.

**4** Roman consuls could appoint a dictator if

  **A** taxes were raised too high by the assemblies.

  **B** the judges could not agree on a court case.

  **C** the Senate ordered it.

  **D** there was a crisis in Rome.

**5** People who could vote in the Roman Republic were

  **A** adult land-holding males.

  **B** adult males and females who owned property.

  **C** free adult males only.

  **D** free adults, both males and females.

**6** What is *one* way in which the governments of the United States and the Roman Republic are similar?

  **A** Citizens elect the head of the executive branch for four years.

  **B** A tripartite government is in place, with each branch having separate powers.

  **C** The power to make laws is limited to the Senate.

  **D** Judges have power beyond the courts.

Name _____ Date _____

**CALIFORNIA CONTENT STANDARD 6.7.3**

# Growth of the Roman Empire

**SPECIFIC OBJECTIVE:** Identify the location of and the political and geographic reasons for the growth of the Roman territories and expansion of the empire, including how the empire fostered economic growth through the use of currency and trade routes.

## Read the summary to answer questions on the next page.

| Adding Territories |
|---|
| • Italy: By 275 B.C., Rome had conquered all of the Italian peninsula. |
| • Punic Wars: In 246 B.C., Carthage, a city-state in North Africa, controlled all trade along the Mediterranean Sea. When Carthage tried to move into southern Italy, Rome and Carthage went to war. The war dragged on for over 100 years. During the second war, Carthage was led by the great general, Hannibal. Finally in 149 B.C., Rome won the Punic Wars. |
| • Persia: Even while Rome was fighting Carthage, it was taking lands to the east. Persia, the empire in Southwest Asia built by Alexander the Great, was slowly conquered by the Romans |
| • By 133 B.C., Rome controlled an empire from Spain to Southwest Asia. |

| From Republic to Empire |
|---|
| • Dictator for Life: Roman conquerors brought back great wealth and many enslaved peoples. A large gap developed between the rich and poor. Finally, a general named Julius Caesar won the support of the people. Caesar made himself dictator for life. |
| • Civil War: Caesar was assassinated. His death marked the start of a civil war. |
| • The End of the Republic: Octavian became the ruler of Rome. He took the title of Augustus, or honored one. The Roman Republic became the Roman Empire. |
| • Pax Romana: Augustus ruled the Empire for over 40 years. During those years, Rome was at peace for the first time in its history. This period is known as the Pax Romana, Latin for "Roman Peace." |

| Unity and Prosperity under the *Pax Romana* |
|---|
| • Trade increased because Rome's armies built roads, bridges, and tunnels. |
| • People spoke Latin throughout the empire. |
| • All citizens were protected by Roman laws and used Roman coins. |
| • The Roman navy patrolled the Mediterranean Sea. |
| • Through trade, Rome acquired grain, ivory, silk, spices, gold, and silver. |

Name _____  Date _____

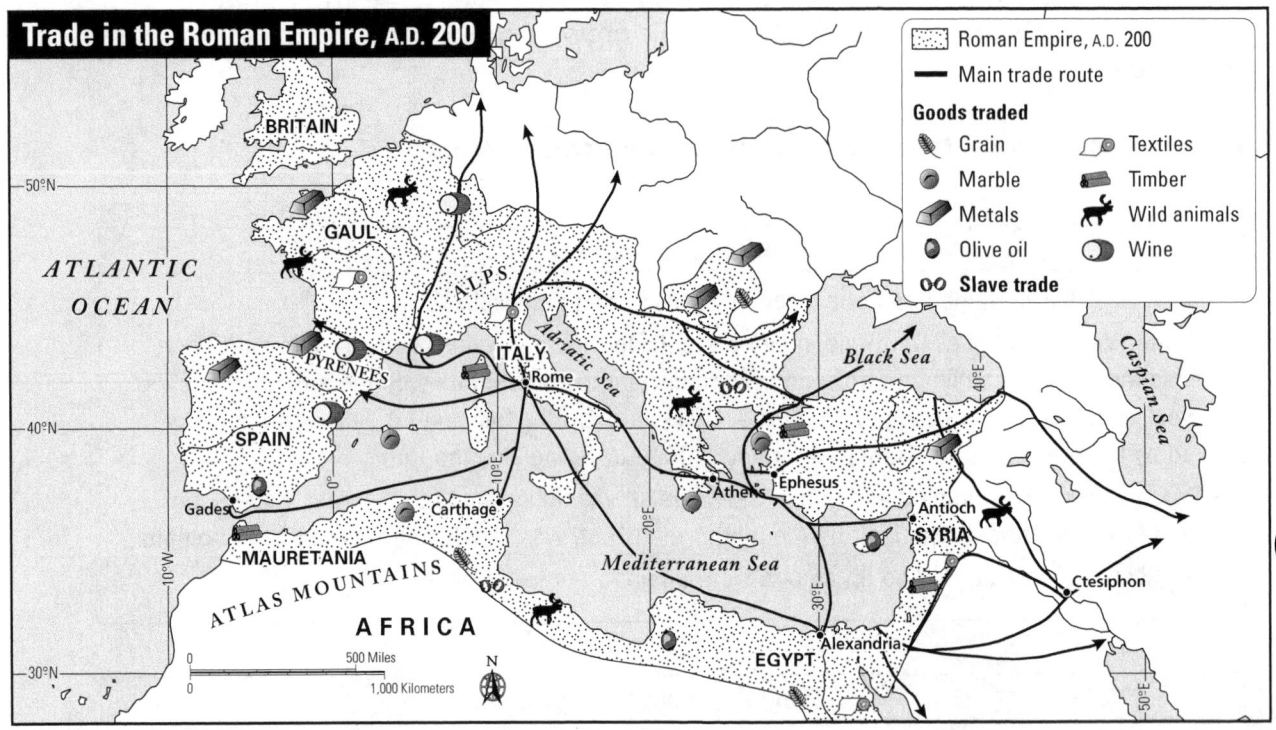

PRACTICE

CALIFORNIA CONTENT
STANDARD 6.7.3

## Growth of the Roman Empire

**DIRECTIONS: Choose the letter of the *best* answer.**

**Trade in the Roman Empire, A.D. 200**

Legend:
- Roman Empire, A.D. 200
- Main trade route

**Goods traded**
- Grain
- Marble
- Metals
- Olive oil
- Textiles
- Timber
- Wild animals
- Wine
- OO **Slave trade**

BRITAIN
GAUL
ATLANTIC OCEAN
ALPS
PYRENEES
ITALY   Rome
Adriatic Sea
Black Sea
Caspian Sea
SPAIN
Gades
Carthage
Athens   Ephesus
Antioch
SYRIA
Ctesiphon
MAURETANIA
ATLAS MOUNTAINS
AFRICA
Mediterranean Sea
EGYPT   Alexandria

0   500 Miles
0   1,000 Kilometers
N

**1** According to the map, when trading, the Romans

**A** used only land routes.

**B** used both land and sea routes.

**C** traded only along the Mediterranean coast.

**D** used only ocean and river routes.

**2** *One* place that provided the Romans with timber was an area near

**A** Alexandria in Egypt.

**B** the Pyrenees Mountains.

**C** the Caspian Sea.

**D** Mauretania in North Africa.

**3** Rome and Carthage fought a war which began as a result of

**A** Carthage moving into Italy.

**B** Rome conquering Gaul.

**C** Carthage conquering South Asia.

**D** Rome moving into North Africa.

**4** Even as Rome was fighting Carthage, Rome continued expanding, so that by 133 B.C., it controlled

**A** China and India.

**B** the Gauls in present-day France.

**C** the city of Alexandria.

**D** Alexander's empire in Asia.

**REVIEW**

**CALIFORNIA CONTENT STANDARD 6.7.4**

## *Julius Caesar and Augustus*

**SPECIFIC OBJECTIVE:** Discuss the influence of Julius Caesar and Augustus in Rome's transition from republic to empire.

### Read the summary to answer questions on the next page.

### Julius Caesar

- **Rome in Conflict:** By 133 B.C., Rome had been at war for nearly 400 years. It had conquered a great empire and life within the republic had changed. Conflicts arose between plebeians and patricians, keeping Rome in turmoil during Caesar's early life.

- **Caesar Betrayed:** Caesar became a great general supported by Crassus, a rich man, and Pompey, another general. Caesar's armies conquered Gaul, fighting for eight years. Caesar's messages from Gaul made some people fear that Caesar would make himself king. By 50 B.C., Crassus was dead, and Pompey had become Caesar's enemy. With Pompey's approval, the senate ordered Caesar to return to Rome without his armies.

- **Civil War:** Caesar ignored the Senate's orders, and civil war broke out between Caesar and Pompey. In 48 B.C., Caesar defeated Pompey's troops.

- **Caesar as Dictator:** When Caesar returned to Rome in 46 B.C., he had the support of the people. The Senate appointed him dictator for ten years. As dictator, Caesar created jobs for the poor, constructing public buildings. He also got laws passed to help the poor out of debt. In 44 B.C., Caesar extended his rule to a lifetime dictatorship.

- **The Plot against Caesar:** A number of senators saw Caesar as a threat to the Republic. Although Caesar was warned, he walked unarmed into the Senate on March 15, 44 B.C. The men who had planned his death rushed toward him with knives. At first Caesar fought, but when he saw that his friend Brutus was among them, he gave in to death.

### Augustus

- **Civil War Under Octavian:** Before his death, Caesar had chosen his great nephew Octavian as his heir. After Caesar's murder, civil war broke out as Octavian fought his rivals for power. Octavian and his enemies clashed at a great naval battle in 31 B.C., where Octavian emerged the winner.

- **"First Citizen" to "Exalted One:"** Fearing the same fate as his uncle's, Octavian at first took the title of "first citizen." In 27 B.C., the Senate begged Octavian to take the title of Augustus, or "exalted one." Under Augustus, the Roman state was ruled by one monarch as an empire.

- **The Roman Peace:** Augustus ruled Rome for more than 40 years. The period of peace and prosperity—the *Pax Romana*, lasted for 200 years.

**PRACTICE**

CALIFORNIA CONTENT
STANDARD 6.7.4

*Julius Caesar and Augustus*

**DIRECTIONS: Choose the letter of the *best* answer.**

**1** Which statement *best* describes Rome during Caesar's early life?

**A** Emperors were only allowed to rule for ten years.

**B** The army of Rome was very weak and refused to fight.

**C** There were frequent conflicts between plebeians and patricians.

**D** Consuls refused to choose dictators.

**2** After Caesar conquered Gaul, Pompey and the Senate tried to gain power over Caesar by forcing him to

**A** fight against Queen Cleopatra in Egypt.

**B** pay huge fines for breaking Roman laws.

**C** admit that he wanted to be dictator for life.

**D** return to Rome without his armies.

**3** Caesar's opponents claimed that he

**A** wanted too much power.

**B** was a poor military general.

**C** wasted much of Rome's wealth.

**D** oppressed Rome's poor people.

**4** After Caesar's death, Octavian had power in Rome because

**A** widespread elections were held.

**B** Caesar had chosen Octavian as his heir.

**C** Octavian was a leader with no rivals in Rome.

**D** people believed Octavian was descended from gods.

**5** At first, to avoid Caesar's mistake, Octavian preferred to be called

**A** exalted one.

**B** first citizen.

**C** servant of Rome.

**D** executive.

**6** Augustus's reign marked a 200-year period in Roman history that became known as the

**A** Roman Republic

**B** Roman Peace.

**C** Augustine Empire.

**D** Roman Democracy.

**REVIEW**

CALIFORNIA CONTENT
STANDARD 6.7.5

# *Judaism During the Roman Empire*

**SPECIFIC OBJECTIVE:** Trace the migration of Jews around the Mediterranean region and the effects of their conflict with the Romans.

## Read the summaries to answer questions on the next page.

### Migration Within the Mediterranean Region

- **A People Apart:** Unlike their neighbors, the Jews believed in only one God. People living among or near the Jews often saw them as a "people apart" because the Jews worshipped God according to the laws of their holy book— the Torah, or Hebrew Bible.

- **Egypt:** In Egypt, Jews were ensalved. Sometime around 1250 B.C., Moses led the Jews out of Egypt back to Canaan, the Jewish homeland.

- **Jewish Kingdom:** Around 1020 B.C., Saul united the Jews. Saul was the first king to rule Canaan, or Judea. Here the Jews built the great temple in Jerusalem.

- **Babylonian Captivity:** In 586 B.C., the Babylonians captured Jerusalem and destroyed the temple. The Jews were forced into exile, or homeless wandering, in Babylon.

- **Return to Judah:** Jewish exile in Babylon ended in 538 B.C. when the Persians conquered Babylonia and allowed the Jews to return.

- **More Conquests:** After their return, the Jews were ruled by Alexander the Great and by rulers from Egypt and Persia. In 142 B.C., the Jews gained independence.

### Conflict Between Jews and Romans

- The Romans conquered Judea in 63 B.C. Romans did not force the Jews to worship Roman gods. Still, many Jews wanted the right to live by Jewish laws.

- Jews in Jerusalem revolted against Rome in A.D. 66.

- It took the Romans seven years to put down the revolt. During this war, Rome destroyed the great temple in Jerusalem.

- A small group of Jews kept up resistance for over three years. Surrounded in a mountain fortress called Masada, they took their own lives rather than surrender.

### The Diaspora

- After the destruction of the Jewish temple, the Romans force many many Jews out of Judea.

- Some Jews stayed in Rome, but most went into exile. This movement of Jews is part of the Diaspora, a Greek word meaning "scattered."

- By about A.D. 500, there were Jewish communities in more than a dozen cities throughout the Mediterranean. For example, Jews lived in Egypt, Turkey, and Spain.

Name _____  Date _____

**DIRECTIONS: Choose the letter of the *best* answer.**

**1** **One** way in which Judaism differed from Roman religion was that

  **A** Jews worshipped a single god.

  **B** Romans did not build temples for their gods.

  **C** Romans would not allow others to worship their gods.

  **D** Jews had no set of rules to follow.

**2** At the beginning of Roman rule of Judea in 63 B.C., how did Roman rulers treat the Jews?

  **A** Romans enslaved the Jews.

  **B** Romans forced Jews out of Judea into Babylonia.

  **C** Romans let Jews govern themselves.

  **D** Romans allowed Jews to worship their own God.

**3** A revolt by Jews in Jerusalem against Roman rule in A.D. 66 resulted in

  **A** the destruction of the great temple.

  **B** a peace treaty between the Romans and the Jews.

  **C** the conversion of many Jews to Christianity.

  **D** Romans forcing the jews to worship Roman gods.

**4** After the Romans overtook Jerusalem, where did a small group of Jews keep up resistance for three years?

  **A** the ruins of the temple

  **B** a mountain fortress called Masada

  **C** Babylonia

  **D** in exiled wandering

**5** Which event increased the Jewish Diaspora?

  **A** After the Jews built the first temple in Jerusalem, the Babylonians conquered them and forced them to leave their homeland.

  **B** Led by Moses, Jews left Egypt and returned to Canaan.

  **C** After the Babylonian Captivity, the Jews were conquered by Alexander the Great.

  **D** After the Romans destroyed the Jewish temple in Jerusalem, the Romans began to force Jews to leave Judea.

**6** By about A.D. 500, Jews were living throughout

  **A** the United States.

  **B** the Roman Empire.

  **C** Eastern Europe and Russia.

  **D** the Mediterranean region.

**REVIEW**

CALIFORNIA CONTENT
STANDARD 6.7.6

# Origins and Growth of Christianity

**SPECIFIC OBJECTIVE:** Note the origins of Christianity in the Jewish Messianic prophecies, the life and teachings of Jesus of Nazareth as described in the New Testament, and the contribution of Paul the Apostle to the definition and spread of Christian beliefs.

**Read the summaries to answer questions on the next page.**

### The Promise of a Jewish Messiah

- Jews believed in one God, unlike neighboring peoples. During their history, Jews were often punished for their beliefs by being exiled, or even enslaved.
- According to biblical teachings, God had promised that a Messiah or deliverer, a descendent of King David, would restore the kingdom of Israel and bring a period of peace.

### The Life and Teachings of Jesus of Nazareth

- **The Gospels:** We know about Jesus from four accounts written after Jesus's death by Matthew, Mark, Luke, and John. The Gospels and other writings make up the New Testament of the Bible.
- **The Disciples:** Jesus was born in Bethlehem and grew up in Nazareth. Jesus studied the Hebrew Bible and other religious writings. He began preaching as a young adult. Biblical accounts say he cured the sick and performed other miracles.
- **Teachings:** Jesus preached justice, compassion, love, and the coming of God's kingdom.
- **Enemies:** Jesus angered Roman leaders by teaching that God had more authority than the government.
- **Arrest and Trial:** According to three Gospels, Jesus's followers hailed him as a king when he traveled to Jerusalem. There, Jesus publicly criticized how the temple was run. He was arrested, taken to the Roman governor Pontius Pilate, accused of plotting to be king, and sentenced to death. On a desolate hill called Calvary outside Jerusalem, Jesus was put to death on a cross.
- **Resurrection:** On the third day after Jesus's death, some of his followers reported that his tomb was empty. Accounts of Jesus's resurrection, or return to life, proved to his followers that Jesus was divine.

### Paul and Christianity

- Paul was a Jew whose Hebrew name was Saul. While traveling to Syria, he reportedly had a vision of Jesus. He then began using his Roman name, Paul, and spent his life spreading Jesus's message.
- Paul traveled throughout the Mediterranean area about 40–50 A.D. teaching Christianity.
- Paul argued that conversion to Judaism was unnecessary to becoming a Christian. His ideas helped separate Judaism from Christianity and spread Christianity throughout the Roman Empire.
- Almost everywhere Paul went, he started churches, and kept in contact by writing letters. Known as the Epistles, Paul's letters explaining Christianity became an important part of the New Testament.

**PRACTICE**

**CALIFORNIA CONTENT STANDARD 6.7.6**

*Origins and Growth of Christianity*

**DIRECTIONS: Choose the letter of the *best* answer.**

1 According to biblical tradition, God had promised the Jewish people that a Messiah would

A help the Jews conquer other lands.

B restore Israel and bring peace and prosperity.

C help the Jews become wealthy.

D rebuild the temple in Jerusalem.

2 Jesus of Nazareth was born

A to parents who were Roman citizens.

B during a time when Jews were not allowed to worship God.

C in Israel when King David ruled.

D as a Jew under Roman rule.

3 The Gospels tell the story of Jesus and were written by

A Jesus.

B Mary and Joseph.

C Paul.

D Matthew, Mark, Luke, and John.

4 *One* of Jesus's ideas which angered his enemies was that

A God's kingdom had more authority than Rome.

B Jesus's followers could not become sick or lame.

C the Roman government should be overthrown by force.

D only Jews could be saved and enter Heaven.

5 When followers of Jesus heard of his return to life, or resurrection, they believed that he

A would bring riches to his disciples.

B could not be killed in battle.

C was divine, or a part of God.

D would lead them out of Rome.

6 Paul's letter to the new churches he had established are important today because they

A explain many Christian beliefs.

B document where and when Paul traveled.

C detail the history of Jesus's life.

D show similarities between Judaism and Christianity.

**REVIEW**

CALIFORNIA CONTENT
STANDARD 6.7.7

*The Spread of Christianity*

**SPECIFIC OBJECTIVE:** Describe the circumstances that led to the spread of Christianity in Europe and other Roman territories.

**Read the summary to answer questions on the next page.**

As more non-Jews, or Gentiles, joined the Christian movement, the Romans became alarmed. Some Christians claimed that they should not have to worship the emperor.

## Early Christians Persecuted

- Nero and other Roman emperors (A.D. 64–312) persecuted Christians by killing, arresting, and torturing them, as well as by destroying churches.
- Despite this danger, more and more people became Christians.

## Emperor Constantine's Conversion

- **Persecution:** Like those before him, Emperor Constantine allowed the persecution of Christians when he came to the throne in A.D. 306.
- **Conversion:** In the midst of fighting in A.D. 312, Constantine believed he saw a sign from the Christian God and that he won battles with God's help. As a result, Constantine ended Christian persecutions immediately, made Christianity legal, and returned property to Christians. He also built many Christian churches throughout the empire.
- **A New Capital:** Constantine established a new capital of the Roman Empire in Constantinople (now Istanbul, Turkey) that served as a center of Christianity for 1000 years.

## Christianity Becomes the Religion of the Roman Empire

- **Official Religion:** In A.D. 380, Emperor Theodosius made Christianity the official religion of the Roman Empire.
- **Roman Catholic Church:** Christianity in Roman cities took on a common structure. Priests obeyed bishops, or local church leaders. Roman Catholic tradition says that Rome's first bishop was the apostle Paul. Much later, Rome's bishop became the most important bishop, or pope. This was the beginning of the Roman Catholic Church.
- **Practices:** Some early Christian writers, called church fathers, developed a creed, or statement of belief. This creed featured a belief in the trinity—Father, Son, and Holy Spirit—as one God.

**PRACTICE**

**CALIFORNIA CONTENT STANDARD 6.7.7**

# The Spread of Christianity

**DIRECTIONS: Choose the letter of the *best* answer.**

1  Romans opposed early Christians because the Christians
   A   refused to pay taxes.
   B   did not obey Roman laws.
   C   seemed to challenge Roman authority.
   D   helped other territories fight against Rome.

2  Which statement describes an unintended result of Christian persecution by Nero and other Roman emperors?
   A   More people converted to Christianity, even though it was dangerous.
   B   Christians organized armed revolts in response to the persecution.
   C   Most Christians moved outside the Roman Empire to escape.
   D   Christians became a strong force in the Roman Senate.

3  In A.D. 312, Emperor Constantine converted to Christianity during
   A   a church service.
   B   an epidemic plague.
   C   a famine.
   D   a war.

4  Constantine established a new capital city that served as the center of
   A   Rome.
   B   Christianity.
   C   Damascus.
   D   Spain.

5  After Constantine died, Emperor Theodosius
   A   outlawed Christianity for several years.
   B   tore down the largest church in Rome.
   C   made Christianity the official religion.
   D   sent missionaries throughout Asia.

6  Some early Christian writers developed a creed that featured
   A   ideal life in monasteries.
   B   the apostle Paul as the first pope.
   C   returning property to Christians.
   D   a belief in the Holy Trinity.

**REVIEW**

CALIFORNIA CONTENT
STANDARD 6.7.8

# The Legacy of the Roman Empire

**SPECIFIC OBJECTIVE:** Discuss the legacies of Roman art and architecture, technology and science, literature, language, and law.

**Read the concept web to answer questions on the next page.**

## Art and Architecture

**mosaics**—pictures made from tiny pieces of colored stone

**sculpture**—realistic portraits, unlike idealized Greek figures

**bas-relief**—slightly raised figures against a flat background

**structural improvements**—use of arches, vaults, and domes; able to build taller and larger buildings

## Technology

**concrete**—developed light, strong material

**aqueducts**—provided water to cities

**roads**—built well so soldiers and traders could move quickly

## Literature

**oratory**—art of public speaking and persuasion; practiced by politicians

**philosophy**—duty, reason, and courage are important values.

**histories**—Roman historians were patriotic, detailed writers.

**epic poetry**—Virgil, Ovid, others used Greek form to tell stories of gods and heroes.

### Legacy of Rome

## Law

**equal protection**—belief that law should apply to all people equally; inspired basis of law in U.S. and other modern democracies

**standards of justice**—written standards evolved: all people accused of a crime have the right to face their accusers before a judge.

## Roman Language

**Latin**—official language; united the empire

**Romance languages**—Latin became the basis of French, Italian, Spanish, others.

**word roots**—many English words have Latin origins.

**PRACTICE**

CALIFORNIA CONTENT
STANDARD 6.7.8

# The Legacy of the Roman Empire

**DIRECTIONS: Choose the letter of the *best* answer.**

**1** Roman sculpture differed from Greek in that Roman sculpture was

  **A** ideal.

  **B** abstract.

  **C** functional.

  **D** realistic.

**2** *One* way Roman engineers improved building techniques was by

  **A** building most structures out of wood.

  **B** developing light and strong concrete.

  **C** eliminating many doors and windows.

  **D** limiting structures to two stories.

**3** *Both* Greeks and Romans used epic poems to

  **A** tell stories of gods and heroes.

  **B** argue for their ideas in the Senate.

  **C** prevent other cultures from knowing their secrets.

  **D** conduct business efficiently.

**4** Some of the most skilled orators, or public speakers, in Rome were

  **A** priests.

  **B** politicians.

  **C** businessmen.

  **D** gladiators.

| Latin Origins of Romance Words | | | | |
|---|---|---|---|---|
| Language | Word | | | |
| Latin | pater ("father") | nox ("night") | bonus ("good") | vita ("life") |
| Spanish | padre | noche | bueno | vida |
| French | père | nuit | bon | vie |
| Portuguese | pai | noite | bom | vida |
| Italian | padre | notte | buono | vita |
| Romanian | tatã | noapte | bun | viatâ |

**5** What lasting impact of language in ancient Rome is shown in the chart?

  **A** An official language unified the vast empire.

  **B** Latin words are used today in biology for naming each new species.

  **C** Modern languages in the former Roman empire share common word parts.

  **D** All modern languages are derived from Latin.

**6** A legacy of Roman law present in the United States today is that

  **A** everyone is allowed a court-appointed lawyer.

  **B** rich people are treated more favorably in court.

  **C** the laws offer equal protection for all citizens.

  **D** laws are made with the direct input of all citizens.

Name _____ Date _____

**CALIFORNIA CONTENT STANDARD 7.1**

*The Roman Empire*

**OVERALL OBJECTIVE:** Analyze the causes and effects of the vast expansion and ultimate disintegration of the Roman Empire.

**Read the summary to answer questions on the next page.**

## Roman Republic (509–44 B.C.)

### Early Strengths
- Written constitution with three-part government
- Citizenship of free adult males who voted and performed civic duties
- Expansion of territory through wars

### Later Weaknesses
- Growing gap between rich and poor; neglect of civic duty by the wealthy
- Outbreak of civil war

## Roman Empire (27 B.C.–A.D. 476)

### Early Strengths/Rebuilding of Rome
- Period of peace known as Pax Romana; strong army and navy
- Flourishing trade and agriculture
- Unification through roads and common currency

### Later Weaknesses
- Food shortages resulting from poor farming and dependence on slaves
- Constant threats from Germanic tribes along the borders
- Corruption of public officials
- Breakdown in communications and inability of emperors to control vast empire

### Decline
- Division of empire in 285 by Diocletian and reunification under Constantine in 324
- Permanent division into two empires in 395
- Fall of the western empire to Germanic invaders in 476

### The Roman Legacy
- Art forms: mosaics, realistic sculpture, frescoes, public speaking, epic poetry
- Use of vaults, arches, and domes in architecture
- Development of concrete, which was used in aqueducts and roads
- Romance languages (Spanish, French, Portuguese, Italian, and Romanian) from Latin
- Ideas about government: concept of citizenship; principle of equality under the law
- Spread of Christianity

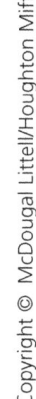

Copyright © McDougal Littell/Houghton Mifflin Company

**PRACTICE**

CALIFORNIA CONTENT
STANDARD 7.1

# The Roman Empire

**DIRECTIONS: Choose the letter of the *best* answer.**

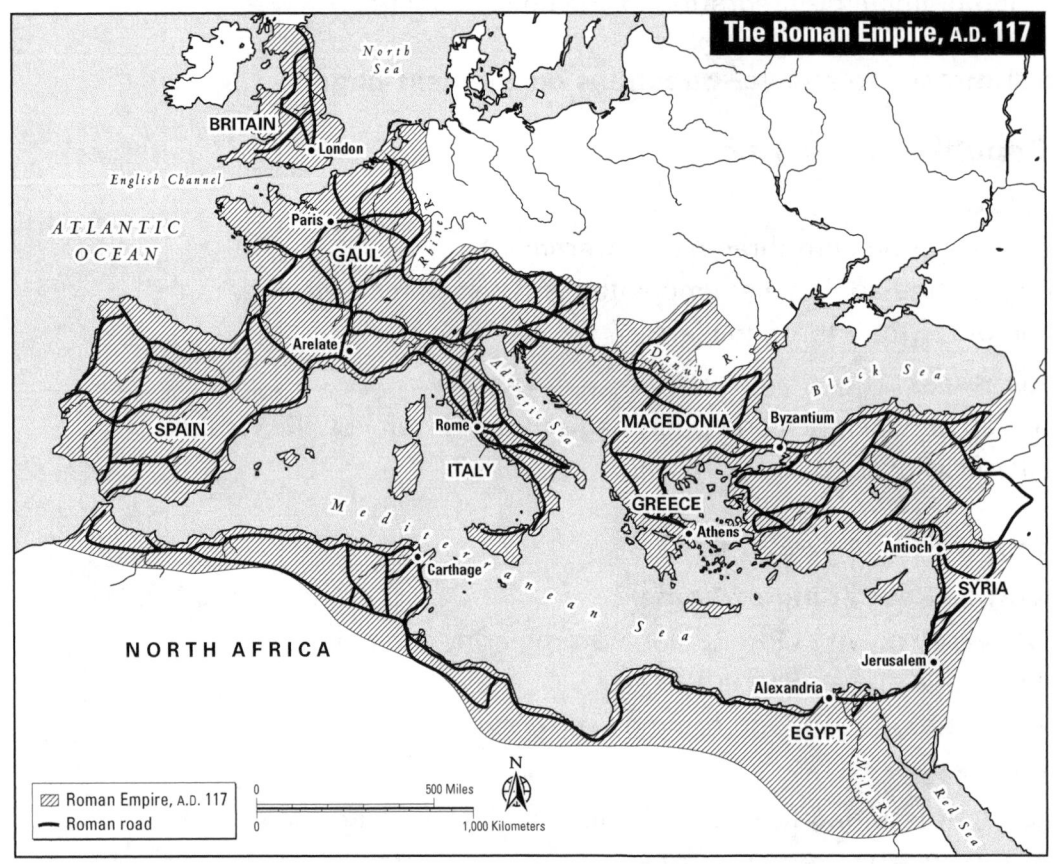

**The Roman Empire, A.D. 117**

Legend:
- Roman Empire, A.D. 117
- Roman road

0 — 500 Miles
0 — 1,000 Kilometers

N

**1**  **According to the map, the Roman Empire included, at its height,**
   **A**  most of Africa.
   **B**  territories on three continents.
   **C**  the Arabian Peninsula.
   **D**  a few of the regions bordering the Mediterranean.

**2**  **What led to the decline and eventual fall of the Roman Empire?**
   **A**  overly powerful emperors
   **B**  economic and political problems
   **C**  religious disputes
   **D**  rebellions by slave populations

**3**  **Why did Diocletian divide the empire into eastern and western parts?**
   **A**  Rome had become too large to govern efficiently.
   **B**  He wanted to separate hostile groups.
   **C**  He hoped to shield the West from Greek influence.
   **D**  The Senate was too powerful.

**REVIEW**

**CALIFORNIA CONTENT
STANDARD 7.7**

# *Early Mesoamerican and
Andean Civilizations*

**OVERALL OBJECTIVE:** Compare and contrast the geographic, political, economic, religious, and social structures of the Mesoamerican and Andean civilizations. (More on Mesoamerican and Andean civilizations is explained in *World History: Medieval and Early Modern Times*.)

**Read the summary below to answer questions on the next page.**

## Mesoamerican Civilizations

### Olmec (1200–400 B.C.)

- Located along southern Mexico's Gulf Coast
- Raised corn
- Built major cities that served as political centers
- Constructed large pyramids as tombs and religious sites
- Organized into classes: rulers; administrators, engineers, builders, artists; farmers
- Worshiped the jaguar spirit in art and life
- Played ritual ball game
- Carved huge stone heads and made elaborate jade carvings
- Developed calendar to keep track of religious ceremonies

### Maya (A.D. 250–900)

- Located in southern Mexico and northern Central America
- Raised corn, beans, and squash using canal system of irrigation
- Built large city-states ruled by kings and linked by trade
- Constructed temples, pyramids, and plazas
- Social classes: king; nobles (priests, warriors); merchants, artisans; farmers; slaves
- Prayed to many gods
- Sacrificed plants, animals, and sometimes humans
- Played ritual ball game to bring rain
- Created pottery, sculpture, jade carvings, murals, and stone sculptures
- Invented zero
- Developed accurate 365-day calendar for religious and agricultural purposes
- Developed writing system using glyphs (symbolic pictures)

## Andean Civilizations

### Chavín (900–200 B.C.)

- Located in northern and central Peru
- Constructed religious centers
- Governed by ruler-priests with farmers making up the majority of society
- Carved stone and created red and black pottery
- Embroidered images into woven cloth

### Nazca (200 B.C.–A.D. 600)

- Located on the southern coast of Peru
- Farmed extensively; built underground canals for irrigation
- Created decorated pottery
- Wove alpaca wool into ponchos, shirts, and headbands
- Produced enormous pictures that stretched for miles on the Peruvian desert

### Moche (A.D. 100–700)

- Located on Peru's northern coast
- Used advanced irrigation systems to support many crops
- Hunted, fished, and raised llamas and ducks
- Constructed enormous temples, including step pyramids
- Made jewelry, pottery, and textiles

**PRACTICE**

**CALIFORNIA CONTENT STANDARD 7.7**

# Early Mesoamerican and Andean Civilizations

**DIRECTIONS: Choose the letter of the *best* answer.**

**1** The majority of common people in the ancient Andean and Mesoamerican societies were

  **A** nobles.

  **B** engineers.

  **C** priests.

  **D** farmers.

**2** Which generalization about the religious practices or beliefs of the early Mesoamerican and Andean cultures is valid?

  **A** Most practiced human sacrifice regularly.

  **B** They worshiped the jaguar spirit.

  **C** Most built temples or other places of worship.

  **D** They played a ritual ball game.

**3** How did the Nazca and Moche adapt to their environment?

  **A** They developed extensive irrigation systems.

  **B** They planted crops that needed little water.

  **C** They hunted and fished instead of farming.

  **D** They relocated to flood plains.

Mayan hieroglyphs. Museo Nacional de Antropologia, Mexico City. © Giraudon/Bridgeman Art Library.

**4** To which ancient culture does the system of writing shown in the picture belong?

  **A** Chavín

  **B** Mayan

  **C** Moche

  **D** Nazca

**5** Why did the Olmec develop a calendar?

  **A** to keep track of religious ceremonies

  **B** to identify when taxes should be collected

  **C** to record the end of one dynasty and the beginning of the next

  **D** to predict celestial events

**6** Which accomplishment is associated with the Mayan culture?

  **A** massive carved stone heads

  **B** underground irrigation canals

  **C** invention of zero

  **D** huge drawings on the plains

4500809868-0607-2020

Printed in the U.S.A